the *pokémon* *is now!*

CHECK OUT . . .

- An in-depth look at the new Pokémon Gold and Silver versions

- Pokémon Stadium—and why it's such a popular game

- A kid's-eye view of the Pokémon TV show and movies

- The mysteries of Missingno revealed—by a fellow Pokémon Master!

- And tons more!

pokémon
future

pokémon
future

THE UNAUTHORIZED GUIDE

Hank Schlesinger

St. Martin's Paperbacks

This book has not been authorized or endorsed by Nintendo or anyone else involved in the creation, manufacture or distribution of Pokémon games, books, or other products, the creation or broadcast of the "Pokémon" television show, or the creation or distribution of the Pokémon movies.

POKÉMON FUTURE: THE UNAUTHORIZED GUIDE

ISBN: 0-312-97758-1

Printed in the United States of America

St. Martin's Paperbacks edition / February 2001

St. Martin's Paperbacks are published by St. Martin's Press, 175 Fifth Avenue, New York, N.Y. 10010.

10 9 8 7 6 5 4 3 2 1

Hey, thanks . . .

I want to thank all of the people who helped out in the creation of this book. First, I want to thank the kids, particularly Tim, who took time out from their busy schedules to share their Pokémon information. Then there's Marc Resnick, who has put up with a lot of totally gratuitous humor and impractical jokes.

And Beverly Willett, who has been a vital link in assisting with the interviews. And finally, to Marc's new assistant, whose name I don't know, but to whom I already owe an apology.

contents

pokémon future

about the kids in this book . . .

If you have read the other books, then you know that a lot of the information in this book is contributed by kids. "So who are those kids, anyway?" you might ask.

Well, they're just ordinary, average kids like you. Some of the kids are older, almost teenagers, and some of them are little and just getting into Pokémon. But really, they're just everyday kids. They go to school, they do homework, and they worry about math tests, just like all kids. They also all love Pokémon.

One thing you should know, though— some of the kids have the same names. So you might see two names that are very much alike, but not quite. For instance, Willy and Will are two different kids. Max and Maxwell are also two different kids. I don't even think they know each other.

One kid, however, Tim, has been giving me stuff since the first book and if anyone is an expert on Pokémon, it's him. Lately he's gotten interested in Missingno and glitches. He gave me so much stuff that it was practically a book by itself. So Tim has his own chapter in this book.

pokémon future?

> "I'm bigger, so I'm more of a fan now. The games are a lot better. I'll be a fan until it stops." **—Adin**

THE BIG QUESTION IS: CAN I EVEN WRITE A BOOK about the future?

Of course I can't.

So why is the book called *Pokémon Future*? I think the answer to that is pretty easy. I think that in a lot of ways Pokémon *is* the future. When Pokémon first came out it proved a lot of things about video games.

For one thing, it proved that the Game Boy was still a good hand-held player. Remember, the Game Boy was already "old" when Pokémon came out. It didn't have a lot of fancy graphics and it didn't have a lot of memory. What it had was Pokémon. All across the country, kids dug out their unused Game Boys from the bottoms of dresser drawers and from under beds. They changed the batteries and plugged in a Pokémon cart and bingo!—bango!—presto!—Game Boy became a huge success again.

Another thing that Pokémon proved is that kids aren't as dumb as a lot of adults may think. Pokémon is a good game, and kids saw that instantly. Of course, there were the television show, trading cards, movies and magazines about Pokémon—but all of that doesn't matter a tiny bit if the game stinks. If the video game stinks, then kids won't play it. That's a fact.

And lastly, Pokémon proved that you don't need a lot of blood and guts and skull-juggling for kids to like a video game. Pokémon did something that no other video game had done before. It combined a Role Playing Game (RPG) with a strategy combat game and, maybe best of all, virtual collecting. Plus, it did it all on the humble Game Boy.

So what exactly is the future of Pokémon?

"I'm still a big fan. I think it's just because I got to play Silver and I think it's cool because there are all these new Pokémon ." **–Roger**

This is what I think the future is going to be for Pokémon. I think that yes, there will be more Pokémon games. And probably more TV shows and movies. Eventually, and this is kind of sad, Pokémon will fade away. All video games lose their popularity after a while. That's a fact. However—and this is the most important part—Pokémon taught everyone a lot. It taught the game manufacturers that kids would play really, really good games. The first Pokémon games took a lot of time to make—seven years—but it was worth it! They are great games. Hopefully the video game manufacturers, like Nintendo, will create more Pokémon-quality games with lots of strategy and challenges involved now that they found out kids will play them.

And I think that kids learned how good a video game will be. After playing Pokémon, bad video games seem really awful. I would bet that there are kids out

there now—maybe even reading this book!
—who want to grow up to design video
games like Pokémon. And, probably, some
of them will grow up to design games.

So, even after Pokémon fades from sight,
it's still going to be around, one way or
another . . .

*"I still haven't decided my favorite between
Lugia and Charizard. My very first favorite, I
guess, was Charizard. Before that I don't even
think I had a favorite."* **—Will**

*"My two favorite Pokémon are still Mew and
Squirtle. I like Mew because he is rare and
powerful and I like Squirtle because he is a
Water-type Pokémon."* **—Tim**

what pokémon has proved to the world!

I WAS SITTING AROUND ONE DAY IN MY POKÉMON pajamas with my feet cozy in my Charmander slippers when I heard "Pika! Pika! Pika!" To a normal person, this would be a little scary—especially since I wasn't playing Pokémon at the time. However, I immediately recognized the sound as that of my Pikachu phone ringing . . . "Pika! Pika! Pika!"

When I answered the phone, it was a concerned parent asking me about Pokémon.

"I'm a concerned parent and what's all this Pokémon stuff, anyway?" the parent said. "You wrote a book about it, so you should know."

"It's actually a totally harmless popular cultural phenomenon based on a variety of disparate though interrelated social and cultural childhood variables distributed and reinforced through a variety of popular entertainment and communication media," I said. "There's also the shared social aspect vis-a-vis bonding through a collective pool of knowledge regarding the game itself."

Feeling pretty good about myself, I straightened the collar on my jammies and went back to doing nothing. I had no idea what I'd said to the concerned parent, but thought I might have a bowl of Pokémon cereal and play with some action figures.

That's what us big-time important writers do all day.

Anyway, the concerned parent did get me thinking. It got me thinking about what is all this Pokémon stuff, anyway? So instead of playing with action figures, I sat down and made up this list. I call it: What Pokémon Proved To The World! (Pretty good title, huh?)

A) KIDS AREN'T STUPID: Pokémon proved that kids all over the world aren't as stupid as they sometimes act. This is, personally, a comforting thought to me, since one of these kids playing Pokémon today might one day be performing surgery on me . . . Oh boy, I hope the kid at least collected most of the Pokémon.

More importantly, it proved that kids had enough brains to recognize a high-quality game when they played it. A great many kids played the game through to their conclusion or found parts of the game—like trading Pokémon—that they really enjoyed.

B) NO FANCY-PANTS GRAPHICS: It proved that you don't need a whole lot of fancy-pants graphics to be a great game and that a totally original and well-designed game will be played by kids. Remember, Game Boy was ancient news when Pokémon came out. I know for a fact that a lot—A LOT!—of Game Boys were rescued from the bottoms of dresser drawers and under beds to go back into action playing Pokémon.

And what made these kids pull out the old Game Boy consoles? It was a video game that was unlike anything anyone had seen before. It was so well-designed and thought out that kids couldn't help but be attracted to it.

C) NO BLOOD, GUTS OR GUNS: I've said this before and I'll say it again: Pokémon is a great game because there is no real violence in it. It's proven, once and for all, that great video games don't have to be violent.

D) GIRLS PLAY VIDEO GAMES: For a long time people thought that girls were not interested in video games. You never saw them playing video games very much. This is stupid, but true. A lot of people thought that only boys liked video games. Pokémon proved that girls will play video games if there is a video game worth playing.

E) LITTLE KIDS CAN PLAY, TOO: It proved that little kids really want to play video games and will play if there are games worth playing that are easy enough. Pokémon was good for this, because even if the little kid didn't get very far in the game, he or she could still have fun trading and collecting.

pokémon dead? don't count on it!

So how cool is this? When Nintendo released the Gold and Silver versions in October of 2000, the games sold more than 1,400,000 copies of the two versions in one week! We're talking about a *lot* of carts there. It's actually a new record!

Funny, but it seems like only yesterday that the original Blue and Red versions were introduced. Actually, it was in September of 1998. And since then, millions and millions of kids have bought them.

"My favorite character was always Squirtle because he's cute. I've got a little holographic sticker of him with a beach ball, wearing sunglasses and sticking his tongue out in a happy sort of way. Pikachu was too annoying, too

famous. Enough, pick someone new. Like some of the birds. I also like Alakazam." **—Adam**

"So far I think Gold is my favorite. It's the most fun. It's different Pokémon, different strategies, different towns. It's just different because Yellow, Red and Blue are practically all the same. And it's fun because it's a harder game than the other ones." **—Colin**

"My favorite game is Pokémon Pinball. It's the most fast-moving game of them all. I never got bored. You never had to walk down one single path for like an hour and a half. Your hands are always shaking. A lot of fun." **—Adam**

"I caught Mew at a giveaway with my friend at a mall in New Jersey. Getting Mew in a giveaway is the only way to get him without Gameshark. Mew can learn any HM or TM and he is #151. Here's a tip for lucky trainers who have Mew: You should teach Mew Hyper Beam (TM15), Fly (HM02), Psychic (TM29), and Tri Attack (TM49)." **—Tim**

a note to parents

NOW THAT VIDEO GAMES HAVE COME TO THE forefront of what is sometimes a very loud public debate, far more parents are monitoring what types of video games their kids play. This is a good thing. For years, the ESRB rating system somehow slipped beneath the radar of many parents. In part, this was due to how parents defined video games. For many parents, video games meant old-fashioned primitive graphics and wholesome, whimsical themes. Pac-Man and Space Invaders come to mind as falling into that particular category.

These parents were shocked to discover the level of violence included in many of the games their children played. The level of violence, combined with developments in technology that rendered realistic images, made the games wholly unacceptable.

However, now that the problem is out in the open, some parents still remain confused or ignorant about the current games. Extremely violent games make up only a small—though noisy—portion of the total number of video games currently on the market. Though, Nintendo, in particular, remains one of the few major video game manufacturers with a large and growing catalogue of wholesome games generally suitable for pre-teens.

With that said, video games, like movies and television and music, should fit into your own, predetermined household standards.

Like it or not, video games are just one of a kid's many entertainment options available today, and this is not going to change any time soon. And, like movies, music and television, their content covers a vast area that ranges from the educational to the distasteful.

Following is a list of five simple things parents can do to monitor and control the games their children play.

A) LEARN THE RATINGS: The Electronic Software Rating Board (ESRB) ratings are accurate and fair. Complete descriptors are included on every video game box for sale in the U.S. Some imported games do not include ESRB ratings and should be previewed prior to letting a child play.

B) SET HOUSEHOLD STANDARDS: Every household has its own standard on what is "acceptable" entertainment. The ESRB ratings, like movie ratings, do have some latitude. While E for Everyone ratings are usually a safe bet, the T for Teen rating can prove particularly troublesome in judging appropriate content. In particular, many shooting and action games rated T may have unacceptable levels of violence. It is safe to say that any game containing a combat or gun theme should be previewed by a parent beforehand.

C) WORK WITH (AND NOT AGAINST) LOCAL RETAILERS: Only recently have retailers themselves become aware of the importance of the ESRB ratings. In the past, many retailers and rental outlets that would not dream of renting an R-rated movie to a pre-teen consistently rented T and M-rated video games to children. This is changing in part because of the publicity the issue of violence in video games has received.

Independent local retailers are usually open to working with parent groups, such as the PTA and other community organizations. The solution might be as simple as alerting and schooling check-out personnel on the ESRB rating system so that they don't rent inappropriate games to kids. Another, more ambitious, solution that has worked in some areas is repositioning appropriate E-rated videos close to the kids' film section to create a "Kids Corner" within the store.

D) KNOW THE GAMES: Reading reviews readily available on the

Internet, reviewing descriptions of the games on the box at the retail outlet, and sharing information with other parents, are all good places to start. However, there is no substitute for experience. Parents should make an effort to play the games that their kids play or want to play. This is the most effective way to ensure that the games fall within household standards. If possible, parents should even play along with their kids once the games have been approved. Competing with your child offers an interaction you can't get from watching a movie or television show together. And if the new games leave the parent a little befuddled, there are currently dozens of "classic" video game titles available on the market that can be assured of recalling a certain nostalgia for the parent.

E) TALK TO OTHER PARENTS:

Communication between other parents can help you avoid inappropriate games in the marketplace. And lines of communication, when done diplomatically, can also help keep your child away from games that don't fit within the standards you set at home. Most reasonable parents will respect another parent's standards in regard to video game content.

THE MAJORITY OF REPUTABLE VIDEO GAME MANU-facturers submit their games for an ESRB rating. Each video game box should include two types of information to describe the game's content. The first is a Rating Symbol that appears on the front of the box in a small square. The second is what's called a Content Descriptor, which describes the content of the game in a few words. Be sure to review both Symbol and Content Descriptor for all game purchases and rentals.

EC: This means Early Childhood. Not only is a game that is rated EC free of objectionable material, but the gameplay is also easy enough for younger children.

K-A: stands for Kids to Adults. Content of these games is suitable for kids six years and older. However, they may contain some mild violence and jokes. This rating is found on games that were released prior to 1998. The E for Everyone rating replaced the K-A rating after 1998.

E: The new rating which replaced the K-A. All Pokémon games are rated E.

T: for Teen. These games are suitable for those who are 13 years and up, according to the ESRB. However, household standards may vary on individual games. T games may include some violent content and strong language.

M: for Mature. These games should not be played by anyone under 17 years old. They almost certainly include violence and strong language. They may also include adult situations.

AO: Adults Only. No one under 18 should be allowed to play these games.

Rating Pending: The game was released prior to final ESRB decision. Subsequent copies of the game will probably include rating.

this ain't no baby video game guide!

IF YOU'VE READ THE OTHER VIDEO GAME BOOKS, then you know this guide is different from all the others. For one thing, I've tried to make this guide funny and interesting to read. Like the other books, I've put in a lot of jokes and stupid stuff to make it more interesting. A lot of the guides you see out there are all business. They are very technical, which is fine, but they are also written in a serious tone. I think video games should be fun and that video game guides should be fun as well.

Also, you won't find any walk-throughs in this guide. I don't like walk-throughs. I know I've said that before in the other guides, so if you've read this before, then just skip this paragraph. The reason I don't like walk-throughs is that they are a map.

Kids buy the game and they buy a walk-through and then just follow the map through the game. In my opinion, that takes a lot of the fun out of the game. Video games—especially the Pokémon games—should be explored. You should feel like you played the game and learned how to play the game.

So what I've tried to do in this book—and the other books—is to give kids an idea of what the game is about and a few hints that will give them a little help to get over the tough spots. Plus I've tried to make it funny.

In this book, I've tried to cover the newest Pokémon games—the Silver and Gold versions. I've also added stuff on some of the other games, like Pokémon Stadium and Pokémon Puzzle League. Finally, I've tried to give kids an idea of what Pokémon is about and to try to get them thinking about why they like it.

gold and silver versions

System: Game Boy Color (GBC)
ESRB Rating: E for Everyone

"Pokémon Gold and Silver and Stadium are my favorites because, first of all, Gold and Silver are new and different and kind of like fun. Pokémon Stadium because there's more than just playing the game, there's Kid's Clubhouse and trading and you play wacky games that are fun." **—Adin**

GOLD AND SILVER REVIEW

Well, the Gold and Silver versions of Pokémon are finally out. And they were worth the wait. Sometimes when a video game manufacturer brings out a new game based on a previous hit, the new game is really junky. In fact, to call some video games sequels is wrong because they are often junk. I won't mention any specific games, but you know the ones I'm talking about. You've probably played a couple of them.

Well, the Gold and Silver versions are not junk. In fact, they are really, really good. This is one time when the sequel is as great as the opener. Gold and Silver are well-thought-out and exciting video games. Even for kids who had Red and Blue down cold and thought there were no more Pokémon challenges, the Silver and Gold versions will really challenge them.

"Probably Silver version is my favorite game because it's keeping me in my room for about 20 hours, but not straight. Because it's always like a big puzzle and it almost never ends. It draws you in but it gives you more and more. You go into a city and you want to get into a building, but it doesn't let you go into it so you have to do something else to get into it. When you do that something else to get it, you have to do something else to get something in the building." **—Will**

"I'm up to the second trainer in Gold. I've played Silver more than Gold because I'm

trying to make my Togepi evolve. Gold is hard.
Harder than Silver."   **–David**

The question that a lot of kids are asking is: Are Gold and Silver better than the Blue and Red versions?

The answer to that is simple: It all depends which one you like best! If you like the Gold and Silver versions better, then they're best. If you liked the Blue and Red (or Yellow!) versions, then they are the best ones to you. There is really no way to measure best when it comes to a great game like Pokémon. And that's a good thing.

There is one thing that I can tell you. The Gold and Silver versions have a lot more stuff in them. There are more Pokémon, more objects and just plain more to think about. All of this new stuff can make the game a little harder. Plus, the Gold and Silver versions will require you to use all the skills you developed playing the Red, Blue and Yellow versions.

"Gold is more challenging than Red, Yellow and Blue. You can guess what you're going to catch in the other games, but not in Gold. Yellow, Red and Blue are more predictable than Gold."   **—Colin**

"Silver it's double the rest of the games. Instead of eight towns, now they have 16 towns. New Pokémon in the game. The day and night thing is pretty interesting because once in a while people ask you what time it is and if you're not looking at the clock, you can give them a time and that time will change. If it's daytime, and you tell them it's 12 o'clock at night, it will become 12 o'clock at night. Probably the new Gym Leaders are the coolest thing because pretty much you see the old Gym Leaders and the new Gym Leaders and each has a different difficulty level. And they have different level Pokémon. They have all these new Pokémon that you've never seen before."   **—Will**

"Pokémon Silver is my favorite because it has lots of new Pokémon and they're rare Pokémon. You can't catch them in the regular versions—Red, Blue and Yellow. My favorite character is Togepi. This Professor gave me an

*egg in the game then, when I started playing,
I was at the second trainer, he started to hatch
and that's when I got Togepi. He's my favorite
because he has strong attacks like Metronome."*

—David

WHAT'S NEW? (Glad You Asked!)

Right from the start, before you catch your
first Pokémon, you'll notice the new stuff.
It's actually pretty obvious. There is new
equipment, new places to go and new
adventures. Plus there is new stuff all the
way through the game.

*"In Silver and Gold, when you first start the
game, your house is bigger than the house
they have in Red, Blue and Yellow. You have
a bigger room and you have a kitchen."*

—David

*"In Gold (and Silver) you can talk on the
phone. You have a personal radio. With the
phone you can call people and people call
you. Your mother buys you stuff in this game.
You can listen to music on your personal
radio. I've heard one song so far. I only started the game three days ago so I bet there's*

more stuff. It's cool that the badges spin around. I think that's cool." **—Colin**

"The new creatures are pretty much the same as the Red, Blue and Yellow, but they have different attacks sometimes . . . There's a new Professor Elm and he's kind of funny. He keeps calling you and wanting you to come back to the start of the game, where he lives, to show him stuff." **—Adin**

"Gold and Silver are my favorite because of lots of new stuff and not like Yellow like the same Pokémon and Gym Leaders. You now have different Gym Leaders, different cities and different Elite Four. The new Pokémon are definitely different. I wouldn't say they're better or not but I would say that they're a whole lot more interesting because they're new." **—Max**

THE POKÉ PACK: With the new pack you don't have to find a PC to organize your stuff. You can put almost everything you need in the pack's different compartments. You can use the pack to store Poké Balls, potions, TMs and HMs and whatever else you find along the way.

poké tip: *Use the SEL button to access items quickly. With an item filed in the SEL button mode you can just press SEL and get that item. It can save a lot of time, and it's easy.*

"First of all you have the cell phone that you call up all your buddies in the game with. You have the Pokédex, that's new—it has an enhanced version of the Pokédex. It has a squirt bottle and, if you see, sometimes there's really rare Pokémon you see just standing there, if you squirt it with the bottle, you get to battle it and try to catch it. A lot of new TMs—items you use to teach your Pokémon new moves."   **—Will**

"When Team Rocket takes over the Radio Tower you can't do much in Goldenrod City until you beat them."   **—Maxwell**

POKÉ GEAR: This is a nifty totally new game gizmo that you'll only find in the Gold and

Silver versions. At the beginning of the game the Poké Gear is only a watch and a phone. These are really helpful devices, because with the phone you can call other characters to brag or to ask for help. The watch is also very helpful because in this game time matters!

That's pretty good, but you can expand it as you go through the game for additional functions. These other functions include a Town Map you can use to find out where you are in the game, and a Radio that comes in real handy, too. Remember, the Poké Gear is different from the Pokédex! That means, the "Gear" doesn't replace your "Dex" functions!

"I heard about the radio from my friends and it sounded good. I really wanted to use it, but then it didn't work. Then I got the Radio Card from the woman at the desk at Radio Tower after answering some easy questions." **–Willy**

"You also have a cell phone and sometimes you get phone numbers from beating trainers and you get your mom's phone number in the beginning and you get Professor Elm's. And if

you get a trainer's phone number they always talk about how their Pokémon are so good and how they want to battle you again." **–Roger**

poké tip: Listen to the Radio for useful news and talk to trainers, Professor Elm and others you meet along the way. They have useful advice!

"I found the best way to catch the Rare types in the Gold and Silver is to trade phone numbers with Gym Leaders. They can give you advice about where and when to find them."

–Maxwell

"There's like a new attack in Silver—drink milk. It re-heals your Pokémon's health. One of my favorite new attacks is the flame wheel. It's a fire attack that takes away a lot of damage, but it may burn the Pokémon. It burns your opponent." **–Will**

"There's a Pokémon (in Silver) called Quilava who evolves from one of the first Pokémon you get. He can learn a lot of different moves. He can learn a Grass move, a Fighting move. He can learn a Fire move. He can learn lots of *different moves. There's one trainer called Leader Whitney and she has a Pokémon named Milktank and it has this attack called roll-out. And every time it does that, it does more damage. It's good because if you don't kill it fast enough it'll keep on doing more damage and it'll be unstoppable. Milktank is on Level 20 so I raised my Pokémon to high levels and Quilava is my best Pokémon and Milktank is the other Pokémon for backups."* **—Roger**

"You have a phone on your Poké Gear. And you can get people's phone numbers. There's somebody called Wade the Bug Catcher. He calls you up for a Bug Catching competition where you have to catch the strongest bug Pokémon and you have a time limit of 20 minutes. You can cut it down to whatever you want, but you have a maximum time of 20 minutes. I came in third both times. They're usually held on weekends. He called me up on the first day I got the game." **—Max**

THE CHARACTERS:

"All the Gym Leaders are different from the old game. Gym Leaders are the same in Gold and

Silver. My favorite Gym Leader I'd say was the last Gym Leader, Claire, and she uses dragon Pokémon." **–Max**

"I like Silver the best because it has really cool Pokémon in it, like Hopip. I have a badge in it, too." **–Nina**

"My favorites in battle are Lugia, Feraligatr, Blastoise, and Mew because I like using Psychic and Water Pokémon." - **–Raymond**

"My favorite characters are Totodile, Lugia, Chikorita, and Charizard. They are my favorites because they are powerful in battle." **–Aaron**

poké tip: Holding is a new feature in Gold and Silver. Pokémon can hold items, like Berries, to heal themselves in battle. But they can hold other items, too. Try trading Pokémon who are holding notes.

MOM: Mom, what are you doing here? Your mom plays an important part in these new games. Whenever you win money in the game, send some back to Mom. She'll save it for you. Remember, when your

Pokémon faint in battle, you lose money. If it's with Mom, then it's safe!

PROF. OAK: He's back and he's even more useful in providing information than in the Blue and Red versions.

PROF. ELM: Even though he's young, he has some good information on Pokémon, especially evolving them. Be sure to visit him!

GYM LEADERS: There are a bunch of new Gym Leaders for you to challenge in the Gold and Silver versions. You didn't think you were going to go up against the guys from the older games, did you?

You see, it's like this—there are really two worlds in the new games. The first one is called Johto and the second one is called Kanto. Johto will look really different and contain a lot of new challenges. Kanto will look very familiar if you've played the earlier versions of the game and contain some places that you already know, like Celadon City and Mt. Moon.

poké tip: *Just because Kanto contains some of the places that you know from the Red, Yellow and Blue Versions, don't be fooled into thinking it is the same. A lot—a LOT!—is different than the other versions.*

> "In the Silver and Gold versions, there are two parts to the game. One is when you are into Johto and you have to beat the game in Johto first. Once you beat the second Elite Four two of the guards disappear and then you get to go to Kanto. That is where Blue, Red, and Yellow versions take place—then you have to beat the game there. In all, there are sixteen Gym Leaders, and you get to see Gary on Cinnabar Island and you get to see Ash in Silver Cavern."   **—Raymond**

VIOLET CITY: Falkner uses mostly Normal and Flying types. Defeat Falkner for a Zephyr.

AZALEA TOWN: Bugsy is the Gym Leader in Azalea. Defeat Bugsy's Bug Type Pokémon for a Hive Badge.

GOLDENROD CITY: Whitney's the Gym Leader here. Defeat Whitney's Normal Type Pokémon for a Plain Badge.

ECRUTEAK CITY: Gym Leader Morty will challenge you with his Ghost Types here, and if you win, you'll earn a Fog Badge.

OLIVINE: You'll take on Jasmine's Steel-type Pokémon in Olivine for a chance at a Mineral Badge.

CIANWOOD CITY: Chuck is the Gym Leader here. To win the Storm Badge you'll have to defeat his Fighting Types.

MAHOGANY TOWN: Here you'll be challenged by Pryce with Ice and Ground types for a Glacier Badge.

BLACKTHORN CITY: Clair will challenge you with her Dragon types for a Rising Badge.

"I have had really good luck with the berries in the Gold and the Silver games. The cool thing

*is that the Pokémon use them when they need
them by themselves in battle."*   **—Maxwell**

THE NAMES EXPLAINED

If you remember from the Blue and Red
Versions, the city names were all names
of colors or artist supplies (remember
Viridian City and Pallet Town?). Now the
Pokémon guys have been just as clever in
the Gold and Silver versions. This time the
names are not colors, but mostly types of
plants or trees. For instance:

VIOLET CITY: Violet is a type of wild flower.

AZALEA TOWN: Azalea is a type of bush that
blooms with flowers—very pretty, actually.

GOLDENROD CITY: Goldenrod is a wild
weed that grows in fields. Some people get
hay fever from it.

ECRUTEAK CITY: Teak is a type of very
strong and beautiful wood.

OLIVINE: Olive Vine, get it?

MAHOGANY TOWN: Mahogany's a dark and beautiful wood that is also very strong.

BLACKTHORN CITY: Black Thorn . . .

> *"When you get to the games part of Goldenrod City, you should play all of the games a lot. Some of them will help you win. Also, always look at your chances. Some of the chances of winning are not as good with some games as with others."* **—Willy**

Some of the names of characters will also help you remember things about them. For instance, Bugsy has Bug Types. Morty has Death Types . . . did you know that the word "Mort" in some languages means death?

There are a ton of clever names in the Gold and Silver versions, and a lot of them are the names of plants or things having to do with plants. Ask an adult or check a dictionary to explain names and words you don't recognize. You'll be surprised at how many you find!

> *"Gold is basically the same as Red and Yellow but it was different because there were differ-*

ent Pokémon and there were different people and times and night and day. A lot harder in some ways. You need to keep going back to the place that you started out from to keep going. It's annoying to keep going back, but it's still fun. Silver is good. It's different and it's cool. There are slightly different Pokémon. They look slightly different and it's slightly easier than the Gold game. I prefer Gold because it's more fun. Sometimes Gold is more fun because it's harder . . . I started out with Silver and then I played Gold for a bit and then I kept on playing Gold."   **–Adin**

TWO NEW TYPES!

"Lugia is my first favorite but I still have old favorites: Blastoise, Charizard, Venusaur, Magmar, Zapdos, Articuno, Moltres, Mewtwo, Mew, Dragonite and Electabuzz."   **–Greg**

There are two new types of Pokémon in the Gold and Silver versions. They are the Steel and Dark Types. These can be powerful Pokémon if you evolve them right.

However, there are also a ton of new Pokémon to catch, evolve and battle.

"The new creatures are cool and much stronger than the old ones. Pikachu, Bulbasaur and Squirtle . . . They're my old favorites. I like the way the new Pokémon look. I want to catch the strongest Pokémon in the Silver version–Lugia." **–David**

THE CLOCK

"It's dark playing at night. You get different Pokémon. You can get certain Pokémon at night that you can't get in the day. I never seem to get night when I want it to be night; that always annoys me. I couldn't find Hoothoot during the day. My mom found him at night. I found him once at night when I just got him from Mom." **–Colin**

The Clock is one of the most important new features added to the Gold and Silver versions. In order to win the game you have to understand the Clock and how it works in the game.

The Clock is also a calendar. Once you set the Clock it works on the same time that you do. When you play in the morning it will be morning in your game. If you play at night, then it will be night in your game.

"When you walk downstairs in the house your mom gives you Poké Gear. And you put the time and date on it. The game keeps track of it even when you turn the game off. So if you turn it off at 3 o'clock and turn it back on at 5 o'clock in the game, it will be 5 o'clock, not 3 o'clock in the game. You can also put in Daylight Savings Time so it becomes light at a certain time. You can only catch certain Pokémon at night and not in the day." **—Max**

"Some Pokémon show up in the night and some show up in the day. Spinarak shows up more in the night because he's a spider Pokémon. Spiders crawl around more in the night than in the day. Spiders eats mosquitoes and mosquitoes come out at night. There's a Pokémon named Wooper who's usually found during the day. He's a Water Pokémon and he can't see well in the night. There's also a Pokémon named Hoothoot who knows attacks called foresight and that makes his

eyes sort of glow so it's easier for him to see at night. And you find him more in the night than in the day." **–Roger**

"In my Silver version, I set the clock to 7:59. When I went downstairs, my mom came up to me (not in real life, in the game) and she gave me Poké Gear. Then she asked me a question: 'Is Daylight Savings Time over?' Say 'No.' You want the days to be longer in the game. You can find more Pokémon that way. When you get your first Pokémon, you should choose between Totodile or Chikorita because Totodile has the best defense and Chikorita has the best attack power." **–Raymond**

poké tip: Some Pokémon only appear at night. And some stuff you need to do can only be done on certain days of the week. Keep track of time when you are playing. Time should fit into your playing strategy!

"I was about to get one of the Pokémon. I was checking my Poké Gear which has a map, time and radio and telephone in it. I was just about to check it. It was 5:59. So I knew if it turned 6 I couldn't catch it. Then I would have to wait until the next day. It becomes morning at 9 a.m. So I was just checking the time and making one phone call to Mom to see how much money I saved up with her. Then it said $8,729 and then it turned 6 o'clock. I was very disappointed. I would have to wait until 9 o'clock the next day."   **–Greg**

"In Silver you see nocturnal Pokémon at night. Like owls, raccoon, Pokémon. It's gonna change either way and if you see day and night it's not much different. Some things, you get into different places—buildings—at night. In the day, you get into different places."   **–Will**

"In Gold there are eggs that turn into Pokémon because I got one and like it evolved into Togepi. Out of all of them I've seen they look better than the old ones to me. Mostly, the other games I think they [the Pokémon] all looked a little bit similar. These Pokémon are pretty much different. I think Bayleef is my favorite because he's my strongest and I think he's cute. He's different; he's original."   **–Colin**

"The night is more fun because everybody is weird and sleepy. Actually, I play at night most of the time. It's more fun and there are more interesting Pokémon at night. And there are more fun battles." **—Nina**

POKÉMON NOT FOUND IN GOLD OR SILVER

Here are some Pokémon you won't be able to find in the Gold or Silver versions. You have to trade them from Blue or Red or Yellow versions with a link cable. This is not as easy as it sounds. In order to trade with a Blue or Red version, you have to go into the Time Machine. You can find the way to time travel in Ecruteak City's Pokémon Center. But even after you get time traveling trading rights, don't even think about trading some of the new Pokémon from Gold or Silver back into Red, Blue or Yellow. It won't work!

But you can trade Pokémon that appear in both the new Gold and Silver versions and the old Blue, Red and Yellow versions back and forth. You just can't trade Pokémon Gold that only appears in Gold and Silver back to Blue, Red and Yellow.

Here's a list of Pokémon that you won't find in the Gold and Silver versions. You must trade them into Gold and Silver from Red, Blue or Yellow.

1. **Bulbasaur**
2. **Ivysaur**
3. **Venusaur**
4. **Charmander**
5. **Charmeleon**
6. **Charizard**
7. **Squirtle**
8. **Wartortle**
9. **Blastoise**
138. **Omanyte**
139. **Omastar**
140. **Kabuto**
141. **Kabutops**
144. **Articuno**
145. **Zapdos**
146. **Moltres**
150. **Mewtwo**
151. **Mew**

"Traded Pokémon evolve quicker than Pokémon you catch yourself. This is just like in

the Blue and Red versions of the game. So it is a good idea to trade a lot." **—Willy**

"In Silver and Gold, if you shake an item off a tree and give it to this guy, he creates new Poké balls for you like Lureball and Fastball." **—David**

major poké tip: *There are seven new types of Poké Balls in the Gold and Silver versions. These are very special Balls that come from Apricorns that you can find around the game. Once you have an Apricorn, you can take it to the little guy in Azalea Town and he'll make you a special Poké Ball depending on what type of Apricorn you brought him.*

The new Balls are:

1) Blue Apricorns Make Lure Balls: These are good against Water Type Pokémon that you fish for with a pole.

2) Red Apricorns Make Level Balls: Good for Wild Pokémon with Low Levels.

3) White Apricorns Make Fast Balls: Very good against . . . you guessed it . . . quick Pokémon.

4) Black Apricorns Make Heavy Balls: Excellent against huge Pokémon.

5) Yellow Apricorns Make Moon Balls: Very good for Pokémon that evolve with Moon Stones.

6) Green Apricorns Make Friend Balls: Use this with friendly Pokémon. It makes them even more friendly.

7) Pink (or sometimes called Peach) Apricorns Make Love Balls: Use this to capture Pokémon of opposite gender.

"In Silver I guess Lugia is my favorite because it's pretty much the new, strongest Pokémon. It does Water and Flying attacks and almost every kind of attack, but Water and Flying are the most specific. It's a giant bird and it's one of the five legendary birds. And it has black, almost like black feathers coming out of its

back and it has a blue stomach. It has sort of like five fingers on its wings. And the rest of its body is white and at the end of it there is a big tail and at the very tip of it there's two more black feathers . . . Blaine is my favorite Gym Leader because Fire Pokémon is one of my specialties. Probably my strongest Pokémon is a Fire Pokémon. My starter Pokémon was a Fire Pokémon—pretty much what I'm good at in the game." **—Will**

TRADING FROM SILVER TO GOLD AND GOLD TO SILVER AND GOLD OR SILVER TO BLUE AND RED AND SILVER TO YELLOW AND . . . OH, WAIT, I'M CONFUSED!

Sorry, I got mixed up. Let me try writing that again. Hey, I get confused. It happens. Give me a break, will you? It's not like I'm going to be tested on this and it's going on my Permanent Record. So just calm down and let me try writing that again . . .

TRADING FROM SILVER TO GOLD AND GOLD TO SILVER AND GOLD OR SILVER TO BLUE AND RED, AND YELLOW AND SILVER TO ZELDA AND TETRIS AND FOUR PURPLE

PIKACHUS FOR A BERNIE WILLIAMS ROOKIE CARD AND MY COUSIN'S SISTER'S BEST FRIEND'S STINKY SOCK . . .

No, *wait . . . that can't be right. I got confused again. That's really wrong . . . Oh man, now I'm all mixed up. The real answers are: the Battle of 1812; Napoleon, D: All of the Above; and The State Capital of Florida is Orlando. . . . no, wait, that's wrong, too.*

Okay, I'm gonna give it one last try. Here goes . . .

TRADING POKÉMON AND STUFF

(Much better. See, I got it!)

> *"I trade cards at Toys 'R Us at 9:00 A.M. in my hometown. There, I know some of the video-game staff, so I get Pokémon cards there for only $3.45! I also get great friends when trading cards at Toys 'R Us."* **—Aaron**

> *"I like Chikorita and Hopip, Cynquil, Togepi, Mareep and Bayleef. They're really interesting because they have all sorts of qualities I've never seen in the first 150 Pokémon. They also seem a lot nicer than most of the Pokémon in*

the first games . . . I used to just love Pikachu and I didn't like any other Pokémon. Now I think Chikorita is the best. I used to love Squirtle and now I like Bulbasaur." **—Nina**

One of the most fun things about Pokémon is trading. Kids love to trade. Kids will trade baseball cards and football cards. They'll trade pens in school and desserts at lunch. The guys who made Pokémon knew that and built trading into the game.

Now, with the Gold and Silver versions, there's more trading to do than ever.

Just like in the Blue and Red versions of the game, there are some Pokémon that you can find in Gold and not in Silver and there are some Pokémon that you can find in Silver, but not in Gold. That's easy enough, right? However, to make the game really interesting, Pokémon that are not included in the version of the game you have—whether it is Gold or Silver— can be found in not only the Gold or Silver version of a friend, but also in the Blue, Red and Yellow versions.

This can be a good thing. If you already

have a Blue, Yellow or Red version and the link cable, then you can go back into the older version yourself and get the Pokémon you need.

"My mom and I put down the cables together. Then you go upstairs into the Poké Center. You go to the first lady. Then she moves and she goes into this room and then you go to the desk with like a little Game Boy on it. It's exactly like the other game at that point. So you go in, sit down at the desk and start talking. Then you hit A, push the button A. Then you pick the Pokémon you want to trade. It tells you which ones you're trading. You say 'yes' if you want to trade and 'no' if you don't. My mom was on Silver and she gave me Hoothoot. I gave her Bellsprout."

–Colin

"I only traded once in my Silver and Gold to myself. I have traded a Chikorita for a Donphan because I wanted to have all of the three beginning choices in my Silver and I wanted powerful ones in my Gold, because I just started the game." **–Raymond**

"Once I was in a trade for my Level 8 Bulbasaur for a Level 100 Mewtwo—this is a REAL trade I made with the Game Boy, not the trading cards." **—Aaron**

Pokémon Not Found In Gold But Found In Earlier Versions And Can Be Traded

Ninetales
Meowth
Vulpix
Persian

Pokémon Not Found In Silver But Found In Earlier Versions And Can Be Traded

Mankey
Growlithe
Arcanine
Primeape

Pokémon Not Found In Gold That You Need To Get From Silver Version

Donphan
Delibird

Phanpy
Ledyba
Skarmory
Ledian

Pokémon Not Found In Silver That You Need To Get From Gold

Ursaring
Spinarak
Teddiursa
Gligar
Mantine
Ariados

"You have to play the game for a while to get the trading thing working where you can trade with the Red, Blue and Yellow games. I just started trading. Some of my strong Pokémon—Snorlax, my Aerodactyl, Gloom, my Squirtle—I put into Silver. That's all I've done so far. Well, when you go into a Pokémon center and go up the stairs at the end of the hallway, there's a person in front of a giant machine and it says 'Do you want to trade your Pokémon through time?' The

reason it says that is because the game takes place in the future from the Red, Blue and Yellow. It's also called a time capsule. If you say yes she'll bring you into this room and your friends should be in there too. When you go into the room it'll give you a list of your Pokémon and his, your friend's Pokémon, on the other side. And your friend will be there. On the list you choose the Pokémon you want to trade and your friend chooses the Pokémon he wants to trade and then you see a sequence where you see the Pokémon going from one to another." **—Will**

WHERE DO BABY POKÉMON COME FROM?

One of the new and very cool things in the Gold and Silver versions is the way you can get baby Pokémon. If you go to the Day Care Center in Goldenrod City, you can breed two Pokémon. What you have to do is get a male and female Pokémon and leave them with the couple who run the Day Care Center. When you come back in a little while, they might give you an egg. Carry the egg around with you and soon it will hatch into a baby Pokémon.

Also, remember, the Day Care Center is still a good place to leave the Pokémon to raise their levels.

If you don't have two of the same Pokémon that are male and female, then try leaving two of the same type of Pokémon with the Day Care man and woman. This will only work sometimes. A surefire way to breed your Pokémon is leaving one male or female with a Ditto.

Baby Pokémon And their Names

A baby Magmar is a . . . . Magby
A baby Lynx is a . . . . Smoochum
A baby Jigglypuff is an . . . . Igglypuff
A baby Pikachu is a . . . . Pichu
A baby Clefairy is a . . . . Cleffa

poké tip: Some Pokémon are always males, like Tauros, Nidoking and Hitmonlee. And some Pokémon are always females like Nidorina, Chancey and Blissey. And some Pokémon will never breed. Talk to the two Pokémon you leave in Day Care before leaving, to see if they like each other.

STRATEGY

"In Gold there was Foresight and there was Mudslap attacks. Foresight didn't really look like anything. Mudslap it looked like these brown waves wash over the Pokémon. Quick Attack–they disappeared and then they got hurt, and then they reappeared. Difference in the Quick Attack from the other games? The graphics. In the other games, they weren't too good but in this case, they were." **—Adin**

The basic strategy in the Gold and Silver versions is the same as in the Blue, Red and Yellow versions of the game. The Pokémon games are basically Role Playing Games (RPGs)—so you have to explore. That's the whole point behind RPGs, exploration. You have to explore the new Pokémon world, but you also have to explore when it comes to people that you meet along the way. These people can offer you valuable information and items. Here are some very basic rules for playing an RPG:

A) Go Everywhere: Be sure to see everything there is to see on every level that you visit before moving on to the next level. If you can't get into a building, then remember it and try to go back later.

B) Talk to Everyone: Talk to people who answer the doors of buildings. Talk to Gym Leaders that you defeat. It also helps to talk to people you meet along the way more than once. Sometimes a person with not much to say the first time will offer you good advice the next time you encounter them. In the Gold and Silver versions it is very important that you trade phone numbers with the Gym Leaders. They will call you up on the phone. Sometimes they will call to challenge you again, but other times they will call to give you advice about where to catch Rare Pokémon!

C) Try, Try and Try Again: Just because you can't get into a building or find a Pokémon the first time, doesn't mean that you shouldn't try again. Remember, with the new Gold and Silver versions, some Pokémon will only be around at night, and some events only take place on certain days.

D) Remember As Much As You Can: Try to remember the places that you couldn't get into and the items that you had a hard time finding. This will help you later on when you go back and try your luck again.

"At the beginning of the game you get three different Pokémon to choose from. You can choose Cyndaquil, Chikorita or Totodile. It's like in the other versions, your rival's Pokémon depends on what you choose. But your Pokémon choices are all at Level 5. Get the one you choose as strong as you can before meeting rival." **—Maxwell**

"My favorite is Quick Attack, it's really fast. The Pokémon goes up in the air fast and then goes down to attack. It's faster than in the other games." **—David**

stupid poké tip: You don't have a better chance of catching Flying Types when flying in an airplane. And you won't catch Rock Types by going to a concert.

> "The Gold is my favorite because it's got more things in it. It's not like it's hard or anything. In some ways it's easier than Blue and Red in terms of catching the Pokémon. Every few steps you take, a Pokémon pops up. If you fight more, you train your Pokémon more to get better skills, and better skills make better fighting." **—Stuart**

poké tip: Talk to your friends who have the game. They can offer good advice and tips on where to find certain items and Pokémon. Also, in order to catch all the Pokémon, you need to trade. This is particularly true for the Pokémon you didn't choose at the beginning of the game.

> "I chose Totodile at the start of the game, but couldn't find the other two choices anywhere in the wild. So you have to trade with friends to get the other two Pokémon. This is a good

thing to remember. It will save you a lot of time and running around." **—Willy**

poké tip: You can only get some Pokémon on certain days of the week. Hint: Sharp Beak can be gotten on Mondays when Monica gives him to you.

"A lot of people don't do this, but I train all of my Pokémon to the same levels each time. And since my brother, his highest level is 50 and second highest is 33, all mine are at level 42. I've found it easier. It takes a lot longer but it's easier, because when you lose one Pokémon, instead of having a level that's a lot lower and weaker you could have a Pokémon that's just as strong. You don't have to depend on just one Pokémon. I take my time. It was the first time that my brother got ahead of me. But I took my time and eventually got farther than him. One of my friends taught me this strategy." **—Max**

and a difference of opinion on this tactic . . .

"Even though it tells you, you should make all your Pokémon as equal as you can get it, I've learned that if you take one Pokémon and get it really high up—like 20 or 30 higher than the rest—and then you put it at the head of your line, you can beat more trainers than if you have them all at the same level. I learned it through experience." **—Adin**

"There's some really weird stuff in the Team Rocket headquarters. One is the statues. Every time you get close to one, a Team Rocket guy comes out. To defeat this trick you have to turn them off in the computer room. The second thing is, the floor is boobytrapped. If you step on the wrong place, you have to do battle, but then that place is safe. That's good to remember."

—Willy

"In Silver, for example, I brought my Squirtle up many levels by using my other Pokémon to help it out in battle. And then once it evolved I was able to use it, get experience by having him battle by himself." **—Will**

"A really good move to get is the Headbutt—not butt head!—this move lets you bump Pokémon out of trees." **—Maxwell**

HERE ARE SOME TRICKS

> *"In the old games there's something called Zubat. And you can only find it in caves and dark places, but in the Gold version, you can only find it at night. A lot of the regular Pokémon you can only find in the daytime. It seems like you can only find Bird Type Pokémon in the day."* **—Stuart**

Mystery Gift: To activate the Mystery Gift feature you have to go to Goldenrod City and talk to the young girl in the department store. The next time you play the game, the Mystery Gift feature should be activated. You can trade gifts with friends who also have the Game Boy Color or the Pikachu versions and who have done the same thing. The trades are made via the Infrared port in the game. Be sure to line them up correctly! Some of the gifts don't help you in the game, but some of them do. So it's a good idea to use this feature as often as you are permitted by the game.

Berry Treasure: There are a bunch of berries all over the game and different fruits you can get from the weird-looking trees. Some berries work like Health Points (HPs) and some of them work like medicine. And don't forget about Apricorns. A craftsman in the game can make them into special Poké Balls!

> *"Berries are a kind of self-hold poison cure. That means the Pokémon 'holds' the berry and whenever it gets poisoned, it uses the berry to make itself well again."* **—Nina**

Radio Style: Listen to the radio—a lot. You can get valuable information and advice from all the stations!

> *"You can get a haircut for your favorite Pokémon in Goldenrod City. It's true, and Pokémon like to have their hair cut."* **—Willy**

poké tip: *Always listen to the radio when Prof. Oak is on. He has good advice and information! The radio can also attract certain Pokémon to you! Sometimes, however, it will scare off Pokémon.*

> *"When you're in Goldenrod City, you go into radio tower and you can get a radio. I got a radio. And the radio becomes important because every week there's a lucky number channel."* **—Max**

Let Your Pokémon Hold Items: When you go to the Trade Center to trade, let your Pokémon hold the item first. And some Pokémon need to hold items when they are traded to get the most out of them!

Traded Pokémon Evolve Faster: But you already knew that from the other versions, didn't you? Some Stone-Evolved Pokémon do not learn new moves as quickly.

stupid poké tip: *Playing Pokémon in the bathtub will not help you get Magikarp faster.*

> *"When you beat any trainer and get money, send some to your mom. And this is good because when you are low on money you can go back to your house, talk to your mom and she says, 'Is this about the money?' And*

you say, 'Yes.' And then there's a little box
that asks you how much you want to with-
draw. I saved up $33,000 and then I had $100
left . . . She always lets you have as much as
you want. But it's also based on the amount
of money you have. Every time you beat a
trainer or get some money, send a tiny bit to
your mom. But if you save up for the whole
game, it really mounts up. It would help you
later in the game if you lose a lot of money
going against the Elite Four."   **—Max**

JOHTO'S GYM LEADERS

"The Gym Leaders in the new games are
much tougher to battle than in the old games.
They seem to have more Trainers and stuff.
Plus, you have Gym Leaders like Jasmine in
Olivine City at the Lighthouse who have a lot
of Steel Types. This is a new type and you
have to figure out how to beat them. I discovered Fire and Water work best."   **—Willy**

One of the toughest things about the new
Silver and Gold Versions is defeating the
new Gym Leaders. Finding them is not all

that difficult, but it takes a while to figure out how to beat them and their trainers. This is only natural because you haven't "met" them before. But it's all part of the game. Also, the same basic rules apply to the new Gym Leaders that you used in previous versions against Gym Leaders in Blue, Red and Yellow. The basic rules are:

A) Always go into battle with Pokémon that are of a high enough level. Don't take unnecessary chances.

B) Carefully match your Pokémon Types to the Types that the Gym Leader and Trainers specialize in. Incorrectly matching your Pokémon against a Gym Leader is a very easy way to lose.

C) Talk to the Gym Leaders after you win. They may have interesting and useful stuff to tell you. Don't just fight for the badge you need and leave. Remember, Gold and Silver have the cell phone feature. Always trade numbers with Gym Leaders. They may call up and ask for a re-match or give you hints!

> "There are eight Gym Leaders in Johto and that makes the game really tough, because they are all different. But you really need the Badges in order to finish the game. If you don't have the Badges, then you can't finish and get to the Elite Four." **—Maxwell**

> "The toughest thing about battling the Trainers and Gym Leaders is that you can't run when you are losing, like you can with Wild Pokémon. This means that you have to be really prepared before going into battle. I always make sure that I have more than enough Pokémon at good Levels before taking on Gym Leaders and Trainers. Pokémon that are of more than one Type are very good against Trainers I found." **—Willy**

Violet City

Gym Leader Falkner
ZEPHYR BADGE

Azalea Town

Gym Leader Bugsy
HIVE BADGE

Goldenroad City

Gym Leader Whitney
PLAIN BADGE

Ecruteak City

Gym Leader Morty
FOG BADGE

Olivine City

Gym Leader Jasmine
MINERAL BADGE

Cianwood City

Gym Leader Chuck
STORM BADGE

Mahogany Town

Gym Leader Pryce
GLACIER BADGE

Blackthorn City

Gym Leader Clair
RISING BADGE

Indigo Plateau

Gym Leader Elite Four

"I like the idea of Badges. It's like winning something for doing a good job. Plus, the Badges you win from Gym Leaders help you finish the game." **—Willy**

KANTO'S GYM LEADERS

Vermillion City

Gym Leader Lt. Surge
THUNDER BADGE

Cerulean City

Gym Leader Misty
CASCADE BADGE

Celadon City

Gym Leader Erika
RAINBOW BADGE

Fuschia City

Gym Leader Janine
SOUL BADGE

Pewter City

Gym Leader Brock
BOULDER BADGE

Viridian City

Gym Leader Blue
EARTH BADGE

Seafoam City

Gym Leader Blaine
VOLCANO BADGE

THE BADGES AND WHAT THEY DO

Johto:

Zephyr Badge: The main reason to get this Badge is to get TM31 (Mud Slap).

Hive Badge: With the Hive Badge you can control Pokémon up to Level 30, which is a valuable thing. You can also get TM49 (Cut).

Plain Badge: This is a valuable Badge that boosts the strength of all your Pokémon. You'll need it as you continue your journey. Also, there is TM45 which helps attract Pokémon and makes them fall in love, but not always. Only about half the time.

Fog Badge: A great Badge for Advanced Pokémon players. You get to control

Pokémon up to Level 50 with the Fog Badge. This is very, very valuable, especially as you continue to take short cuts and double-back in the game. You also get the Shadow Ball, TM30, which is great in battle.

Mineral Badge: This Badge makes your Pokémon stronger in battle, something you'll need as you start to take on stronger and stronger Pokémon. TM23 is great for attack in battle.

Storm Badge: Pokémon up to Level 70 will obey you with this Badge. You'll need this Badge if you want to get ready to finish the game and meet the Elite Four. Also you can Fly when not in battle. Plus you get the TM01, which is a great punch move.

Glacier Badge: Increases Pokémon stats. A very difficult badge to get, but well worth it. And necessary to finishing the game. This is Waterfall when not in battle. You also get TM16, which is Icy Wind.

Rising Badge: With this Badge you can use the Waterfall when not in battle and all Pokémon of all Levels will obey you. You also get TM24, which is Dragonbreath that can paralyze an opponent. The Rising Badge is absolutely essential for dedicated players.

Kanto:

> *"It was pretty good when I got to Kanto. Some of the Gym Leaders are in different places, like Blaine, who is now on Seafoam Island. But I still knew what to do to defeat them and what the Badges did from playing the other games."* **—Maxwell**

Thunder Badge: Provides a speed and quickness boost

Cascade Badge: Pokémon up to Level 30 will obey you

Rainbow Badge: Pokémon up to Level 50 will obey you

Soul Badge: Increases defensive powers

Boulder Badge: Increases attack strength

Earth Badge: All Pokémon, no matter what Level, will obey you

Volcano Badge: Increases offensive powers

THE ELITE FOUR . . . OR IS THAT ELITE FIVE?

"This really surprised me about the Elite Four. There aren't four Gym Leaders you have to battle, but five. That's a big surprise. Lance is the fifth Gym Leader and really hard to beat. The way I beat his Flying Types was with Electric Types. That worked pretty good, but was still very hard."   **—Maxwell**

Will—mostly Psychic Types

Koga—mostly Poison and Bug Types

Bruno—Fighting Types

Karen—mostly Dark Types

Lance—Flying Types

"There seem to be a lot more Gym Leader battles in the new version. I don't know if this is true, but it seems like there are more. I do know that they are more important to the game. You really need the Badges and the TMs to help you get through the game. Also, the Gym Leader battles seem to get a lot harder as you go through the game. I think this is true, because the TMs and Badges have more power as you defeat the Gym Leaders."   **—Willy**

pokémon stadium

System: Nintendo 64 console
ESRB Rating: E for Everyone
Players: 1 to 4

"In Stadium Blastoise and Pikachu are my favorites and Primeape and Lapras. They look cool. Pretty much equal." **—Adin**

STADIUM REVIEW:

THIS GAME FOR THE NINTENDO 64 CONSOLE system is nothing less than brilliant, marvelous and very, very cool. In case you haven't checked it out, the game has one major feature that really sets it apart from other games. You can hook up your Game Boy cartridge via a Transfer Pak and download Pokémon into the N64 game. You can compete against either the computer or a friend.

So what? Well, for one thing, you get full-color N64 action-type Pokémon on your TV. And better than that, you get *your*

Pokémon on the N64 system. That's what!

When it first came out Pokémon Stadium was a giant hit. If you've played Pokémon Stadium in the past and haven't played it recently, now is a good time to try it again. You'll be surprised just how good a game it is.

TRANSFER PAKS

The whole key to Pokémon Stadium is the Transfer Pak. It's the Pak that lets your Game Boy cartridge interact with the N64 system. You can use either the Red, Blue or Yellow carts in the pak. Of course, the carts have to contain Pokémon, right? If you haven't played those versions in a while or swiped the batteries out of them for your personal stereo, then you have two choices:

A) Get new batteries for the Game Boy and capture some Pokémon in those versions real quick to play Stadium.

B) Play Pokémon Stadium with "rented" Pokémon you can get in the game. There are a full 151 Pokémon you can rent in the game. However, all the rented Pokémon are of a really, really low Level.

poké tip: *Only put the Transfer Pak into your N64 console when the unit is turned off. Don't insert it when the N64 is turned on. You may be sorry, because you run the risk of losing data.*

BASIC FEATURES

THE LAB

The Personal Computer and other equipment in the Professor's lab will become your best friends in this game. It will not only provide valuable advice and information, but it will also keep your information organized. Here are some basic functions of the PC and other equipment in the lab:

A) Research Your Pokémon: Use the computer to find out about your Pokémon. This is a cool way to find out about their skill levels, evolution and even basic data like Type. You'll also find lots of very, very useful information on the Blue, Yellow and Red versions.

B) Make 'Em Move: You can use the PC to rotate your Pokémon for a 360° view of them. This won't help you win the game, but it is a pretty cool feature.

C) At Your Service: You can use the Pokémon Trade Service, it's right next to the PC to transfer Pokémon from your Game Boy to N64 cartridge using the Pokémon Trade Service. You can do this to trade Pokémon with a friend directly on your N64. Cool, huh?

D) Get Organized: Use the PC to rearrange and reorder your Pokédex.

E) Trading: There's another machine near the PC. This is the Game Pak Select Machine. You can use this if you want to store more than one Game Pak on the system. You can also use this machine to learn more about your Pokémon.

"The rental Pokémon are a good feature. There's a full 151 of them, that is including Mew, but to get him you have to wait until the second round and you can't rent him for all battles. Also, there is no Mewtwo to rent, but you can use him if you already have him on your Game Boy." **—Maxwell**

THE TOURNEYS

There are four major Tournaments in the game. Each of these tourneys offers players a chance to prove their skills with Pokémon of different levels. This is really important to remember. Suppose you're playing against a friend who only has low-level Pokémon and you have low and highly evolved Pokémon? No problem, you can play at the tournaments for smaller Pokémon.

poké tip: *Okay, this really isn't a tip, just something you should know. When competing against friends and not the computer, you don't get a trophy cup. Sorry.*

The First Tournament is the Petit Cup. In this tourney you can only use low-level Pokémon. Plus, if you use rentals, you'll have the lowest level that can enter.

Your Pokémon have to be between Lv 25 and 30 and can't be taller than 6'8" or weigh more than 44 pounds. This is a heavy-duty strategy competition. Light, quick Pokémon are your best bet, and you have to match them against an opponent's line-up.

The Second Tournament is the Pika Cup. This competition only allows low-level Pokémon into it. That means between 15 and 20 Lv.

The Third Tournament is the Poké Cup. The other competitions were just warm-ups compared to this tournament. You have to fight four—count-em, four!—tournaments. If you're playing against the computer, that means you have to take on a lot of trainers. This is like four competitions wrapped up into one. With 32 different trainers facing you, it means you're taking on a total of 96 Pokémon. However, you can change your Pokémon between each of the four competitions.

However, these tourneys are a chance to bring out higher level Pokémon. The Pokémon that compete in the tournaments here—called Balls—should be at levels 50 to 55. The tourneys are called:

Poké Ball
Great Ball
Ultra Ball
Master Ball

"I tried to get Mew to compete in the Poké Cup tournaments, but he's not available."
—Maxwell

"One of the hardest parts is in Round 1, Semi-Final Prime Cup Master Ball, where the lab man may use his Rapidash, and when he does, Rapidash can use Fire Spin and you will not be able to attack! Another hard part is in Round 1, Battle 4 of the Prime Cup Master Ball. The guy's name is Gambler, and if he uses his Dragonite, you're in for it! Dragonite will paralyze you and then use Horn Drill! One thing is for sure, you should choose your Pokémon wisely."　**—Tim**

poké tip: *You can get the Dodrio and Doduo Game Boy speeds for faster action. All you have to do is win the first round in either the Poké Cup or Prime Cup to get the Dodo GB. Now the Game Boy game in the Tower goes double speed. When you win both the Poké Cup and Prime Cup you'll earn the Dodo GB. That will double the speed again . . . Cool, huh? The C-right button lets you switch back and forth between different speeds.*

THE PRIME CUP

If you thought that the Poké Cup was difficult, just wait until you try the Prime Cup. Like the Poké Cup, there are four different tourneys that make up the Prime Cup. And, like the Poké Cup, the Prime Cup's tourneys are called Balls. They are:

Poké Ball
Great Ball
Ultra Ball
Master Ball

This is where the guys come out. Every competing Pokémon in this competition is at least at a Level 100. Even the rental Pokémon are at 100.

"I thought you had to win every tournament to get into the Victory Palace. But you only have to win one of the tournaments and your Pokémon will get in. That's good." **–Willy**

"When I defeated the Prime Cup with my Mew, I found out that Game Boy Tower had changed. I went to it, and when I pressed the right 'C' button on the controller, the Game Boy screen went FAST. It is called Doduo Game Boy, and is your reward for defeating the Prime Cup." **–Tim**

poké tip: *Surfing Pika! To get your Pikachu to surf, you have to win the Master Ball Round Two battles of the Prime Cup. Pika has to be one of the Pokémon you choose for the battles. Also, he has to be a Pikachu from your Game Boy and not a rental. In fact, you can't have any rented Pokémon in your party. The Pika must* *have fought in all battles without the Continue being used. And it should not be registered. If you win, the system will auto-matically take you to the beach to surf.*

GYM LEADER CASTLE

Here's another series of tournaments for you, just in case you didn't get enough in the different Poké Cups.

Gym Leader Castle has nine different gyms. They are:

Pewter Gym
Cerulean Gym
Vermillion Gym
Celadon Gym
Fuschia Gym
Saffron Gym
Cinnabar Gym
Viridian Gym
Elite Four Castle

Do those names sound vaguely familiar? They should. And just wait until you see who you'll be fighting. Does the name Brock ring a bell?

poké tip: *This may prove to be a memory test. Names like Brock and Misty are familiar to a lot of players. But those names aren't just in there to be cute, they prefer the same Types of Pokémon in this game that they do in other games. Misty, for instance, likes Water Types. And Brock still likes Rock and Ground Types. You need to know these kinds of things in order to choose your Pokémon wisely and defeat them.*

Now, it would just be too easy to battle a Trainer and maybe a Leader in each Gym. Hey, that's baby stuff! Each gym has three—three!—trainers and a leader. That means that there are a total of four battles in each gym and 36 battles total for the Castle. But in order to move on to the next gym and battle, you have to win. Once you win, you can go back and re-fight them.

"The good thing about the Gym Leader Castle is that you get to choose six Pokémon before each battle. So you have to really choose those first six carefully." **—Willy**

poké tip: *To get an Amnesia Psyduck you have to be nothing less than a Pokémon Master. I mean, this is tough. But it can be done and you do get to transfer the little guy over to your Game Boy. To get Amnesia Psyduck simply Battle your way to Victory Palace and get all 151 Pokémon statues. Easy, right?*

BATTLES AREA

My favorite parts of the game are the battle areas. These are the Free Battle, Event Battle and Battle Now!.

Free Battle: This area lets up to four friends play. You can play with almost any combination of friends, like two on two or three on one, or a lot of other combinations.

Event Battle: This is a two-player only, but you can go back and compete in any of the tourneys in the game, like the Pika Cup, plus you can also set time limits. This is a great practice mode.

Battle Now!: This is a quick battle mode. You can either compete against the CPU or a single friend. However, you don't get to use your own Pokémon. The computer selects for you.

MINI GAMES

"At the Kid's Club you can play mini games. My favorite is Ekans' Hoop Hurl. Get the gold Digletts for extra points. In order to play Ekans' Hoop Hurl, you must have accuracy."
—Tim

There are nine mini games in this larger game, which is great if you get tired of battling your Pokémon. They are also good for little kids, because some of these games are, well, very silly. You can either play the mini games against the computer or with friends. To get to the mini games, you have to go to the Kid's Club and then pick the game you want.

Magikarp's Splash: Using your A-button you have to make Magikarp jump up and hit the counter. The player who hits the counter the most during the game wins!

Clefairy Says: This is a very simple version of Simon Says. Everybody knows how to play that, right? All you have to do is press the buttons in the same order that Clefairy instructs on her teacher-type blackboard. If you do it correctly, then she'll dance along. Mess up and you're in trouble. Miss five times and you're out!

Run, Rattata, Run: This is a simple race-type game. Your character is on a tread-mill-type gizmo where walls pop up with no warning. The idea is to jump over the walls and not run into them. The player who jumps over the most walls usually wins.

Snore War: This is a weird game. You're a Drowzee trying to hypnotize other Drowzees. The trick is to listen to the sound the swinging pendulum makes before pressing the A button. By listening, you can get your timing down better.

Thundering Dynamo: Three Electric Type Pokémon are hooked up to an electric power generator in this game. You have to switch buttons from B to A and then back on time, or get zapped.

Sushi-Go-Round: Even if you don't like sushi, you'll like this game. In this game you use Likitung to invade a sushi restaurant and eat to get points. The player who eats the most expensive stuff by the end of the game wins. Warning: Do not try this at a real sushi restaurant!

Ekans' Hoop Hurl: As any self-respecting Pokémon player knows, Ekans spelled backwards is Snake. In this game, the snake is curled into a circle that you toss over a bunch of poor Digletts. It's a pretty fun ring-toss game. As you toss the snake over the Digletts you get points.

Rock Harden: In this game, you have to break up rocks that come flying in on your Pokémon.

Dig, Dig, Dig: This is Sandshrew's game where he gets to dig for water. It's kind of a digging race. The trick is to keep an even—though fast—pace as you dig.

poké tip: *The mini games included in Pokémon Stadium are a lot of fun. And they are also very easy to play. The button action is very simple. For instance, a lot of the games use the A button and not much else. If you have a younger brother or sister who wants to play video games, but a lot of the games you have are too difficult for them, then these mini games might work. Little kids really like the Sushi-Go-Round. It's easy to play, and it's silly.*

"There are secret codes for Pokémon Stadium, too. If you nickname a Mewtwo 'MeWtWo,' his tail will turn a brownish color. If you nickname a Meowth 'Meowmeow,' Meowth's tips will turn red. If you nickname a Voltorb 'Voltvolt,' Voltorb will turn light purple. And finally, if you nickname a Pikachu 'Pikact,' Pikachu will turn pale yellow. I also found out that in Round 1, Battle 1 of the Poké Cup Ultra Ball, the Biker Guy's Arbok will be gray."

—Tim

when pokémon attack!

IF YOU'RE A KID IT'S REALLY EASY TO GET CAUGHT up in Pokémon mania. All kinds of stuff you can buy. Plus, these are not easy games to play and they can take a lot of time to finish. And . . . there's just so much Poké stuff out there! And a lot of it looks really, really good. As a kid, the things you have to remember are:

A) Getting to the next level in the game or evolving your favorite Pokémon is not more important than finishing homework or doing your chores. Your homework and chores are much more important than a video game . . . even a great game like Pokémon. Yes, homework is even more important than the new Gold and Silver versions.

B) Nobody needs a complete collection of Pokémon products. I know this is difficult to believe, but it's true. T-shirts, action figures and other Poké stuff are a fun way to show that you are a fan of the game or to enjoy Pokémon in another way other than a video game. However, there is such a thing as overdoing it. Too much of anything is never good.

C) Buy smart. Don't buy counterfeit cards and other stuff. A lot of the counterfeit stuff is made really cheaply and will fall apart quickly or may not even be safe.

I know that some kids think this is a stupid section and a dumb thing to say in a book. One kid even said that I only put sections like this in the book to "suck up to parents." Neither of those two things is true. What is true is that video games, like television and music and movies, is an entertainment. It's a way to have fun during your time off from stuff you have to do. And when entertainment takes away time from important things like school work or causes major fights between you and your parents or you and your friends, then it's no longer fun.

pokémon puzzle league

System: Nintendo 64
(Game Boy Color version expected soon)
ESRB Rating: E for Everyone
Players: 1 or 2

"I tried Puzzle League and it was pretty good. I never played a puzzle game before. I played it mostly for the Pokémon stuff, then tried some other puzzle games—Tetris—which was pretty good. If you think puzzle games are boring, then try this one first." **—Maxwell**

PUZZLE LEAGUE REVIEW

POKÉMON PUZZLE LEAGUE IS ONE OF THOSE games that Pokémon fans either hate or love. There's probably not going to be a lot of middle ground with this one. I'll tell you why. Puzzle League is, well, a puzzle game. If you like puzzle games and like Pokémon, then you're going to like this one. If you like Pokémon, but don't like puzzle games, well, you might not like this game. This is a puzzle game first and a Pokémon game second. According to those who know—and you know who you are—Pokémon Puzzle League is based on the same engine as Tetris Attack. And Tetris, as all you game fans know, is one of the great puzzle games of all time.

So if you have never seriously played a puzzle game, but want to try, then this is the perfect game to start playing.

This is a one- or a two-player game. And for all you puzzle game fans out there—it's a lot—I mean a *lot*—like Tetris Attack. The bonus here is that it's a 3-D version, which is pretty cool.

The object of the game is very simple— but the winning of the game is very difficult. So take some time to get used to playing. And take a lot of time if you want to get good enough to win.

To play the game you just have to line up blocks of the same color in your slot. Line up three or more similar blocks and they vanish. This is a good thing, because more blocks are being added all the time and if your stack reaches the top, then you lose.

When you play against another player

and not the computer, then you are playing on a split screen. The object is to line up combinations which are then transferred to your opponent's side of the screen.

If you're one of those people who has never played a puzzle game because they look "thin" with only one thing to do, then this game will prove you wrong. Although the basic play of the game never changes, there are six play modes in this game, plus lots of tricks.

In single player mode, the basic idea is to defeat 16 Pokémon Trainers. The other modes are: Stadium, Puzzle University, Mimic Mansion, Pokémon Spa, Time Zone and Marathon.

Mimic Mansion: This is basically a training mode where you copy moves at a very slow pace. If you have never played a puzzle game before, then start here.

Marathon: Just keep clearing your area for a high score. This is an excellent practice mode. By using combos you can freeze a stack for a little while.

Time Zone: This is basically the same get-the-highest-score-you-can game that you play in Marathon, except there is a time limit.

Spa: This mode is divided into multiple stages. To win each stage you must clear the panels. Each time you clear a panel you get to advance to the next stage.

Puzzle University: This is an interesting variation. Instead of playing against the clock, you have to finish clearing the panels in a set number of moves. There are three different levels on this mode.

Stadium: In this mode you take on a variety of computer opponents as if they were another person. This is an excellent way to train for two-player play.

SOME PUZZLE TRICKS

Jigglypuff Sings!: Successfully complete a long combo or chain and the game will pause—and Jigglypuff will sing! If you complete a long combo, he'll sing for a long time.

Need For Speed: First win at Time Zone and then go back to the Title Screen and Hold Z and press B-A-L-L. Then go to Marathon and you can select a super-fast game with the speed select feature.

Get All Trainers: First win the Spa round, then you can get all the trainers from two-player mode to go to the Trainer Select Screen and press L + R + Z ON BOTH CONTROLLERS!

"To get Mewtwo you have to beat the game in the S-Hard level. Then you can skip all the other stuff and get right to Mewtwo. To do this you have to hold Z and press B, Up, L, B, A, Start, A, Up, R. When you start the game, it will be on the Mewtwo level." **–Maxwell**

new and improved pokémon glossary!

Animé: A Japanese cartoon, such as Pokémon, or Sailor Moon. Animé is different than typical American cartoons in the artwork used, and also appeals to a wider audience than American cartoons. In Japan, animé is also very popular with adults, and full-length animated movies are also common.

Apricorn: An item similar to Berries that are found in the Gold and Silver versions. However, unlike Berries, they can be crafted into Poké Balls, like the Level Ball, Lure Ball, Love Ball, Moon Ball and Friend Ball. Each of these special Poké Balls has different powers.

Ash: Ash Ketchum, a young boy and the hero of the Pokémon saga.

Badges: You win Badges during the game play when you do something good. There are eight different Badges in the game, like the Boulder Badge, the Earth Badge and the Rainbow Badge. You will need Badges to win the game. See the section on Badges for complete details of what powers they give you and your Pokémon Party.

Berries: Items found in the Gold and Silver versions that restore HPs.

Booster Pack: A pack of Pokémon trading cards that include 11 individual cards ranging from the Common to the Rare. Serious players of the game buy boosters to customize their sets while kids who trade will buy boosters looking for valued cards.

Boss: Video game slang for the bad guy you have to fight. The Bosses in Pokémon are Junior Trainers and Gym Leaders.

Some Bosses are powerful, like the Gym Leaders. Others Bosses are less powerful, like the Junior Trainers.

Brock: A trainer and opponent in the video game, but a friend to Ash and Pikachu in the TV show. The same is true for Misty.

Cable Club: The Cable Clubs are located in the Poké Center. You can go there to either trade Pokémon or challenge a friend to battle. You must go to the Cable Club to trade or fight even if you are using a Color Game Boy with infrared connection.

Cart: Short for the word "Cartridge." You may also see or hear the word game-cart, which is a "game cartridge." Inside the cartridge, which goes into your Game Boy, is the software (computer language) that holds your Pokémon adventure. You wouldn't think that such a little cartridge could hold so much fun, would you? The words "cart" and "cartridge" are also used to describe "console game" software. Console games are the ones you play with a system like Nintendo 64 and hook up with your television.

Colosseum: An arena where you can battle friends by linking two Game Boys together.

Common: In Pokémon the word "Common" means that there are a lot of them. Pokémon that are easy to find, and a lot of which exist in the game, are said to be "common." Pokémon that are difficult to find, and there are very few of them, are called "Rare."

Elemental Stone: There are five different stones that Pokémon need to evolve. They are Water, Moon, Thunder, Fire and Leaf Stones. You can simply buy them in the Celadon store or find them in Item Balls. The Moon Stone can be found in dungeons.

Elite Four: You will encounter the Elite Four near the end of the game. In fact, the Elite Four are the four biggest battle challenges of the game. They are four trainers: Lorelei, Bruno, Agatha and Lance. All have Pokémon with Levels above 50! And each one specializes in a different Type of Pokémon.

Elm (also Prof. Elm): A younger Professor Oak-type character who is also an expert on Pokémon. You can find him in the Gold and Silver versions.

Evolve: When a Pokémon changes (grows) into another form through experience. Evolved Pokémon are stronger and better fighters. However, not every Pokémon evolves. The ones that don't evolve into anything else are more rare and valuable.

EXP (Experience): A Pokémon becomes more skilled in battle and can even evolve when its experience level rises. With each battle your Pokémon will become more experienced.

Faint: What a Pokémon does in battle if it is not up to fighting an opponent.

FAQ: This is a common term used in video game books or Internet sites. FAQ stands for Frequently Asked Questions. It's pronounced like the word "facts," so it sounds like what it is.

GameCube: You might be hearing a lot about the GameCube in the coming months and next year. This is the new mega-powerful console system that the company once called the Dolphin. It's set to be released in Japan in the fall of 2001 and in the U.S. in the summer of 2002. Will there be a new Pokémon game for the GameCube? Who knows? But if Pokémon remains popular, then the chances are very good.

GB: Short for Game Boy.

GBC: This is short for Game Boy Color.

Game Pack (also Game Pak, and just plain Pak): This is the game cartridge that contains the software that *is* the game. The Game Boy "reads" the information stored in the cartridge depending on what buttons you push to play the game. The words Game Pack, Pack and Pak are also used to describe "console game" software.

Gary: Your main rival in the game and Professor Oak's grandson.

Glitch City: a glitch that happens through a number of steps going in or out of the Safari Building (for more information, see "Tim's Missingno Chapter").

Gym: Found in the cities and towns, Gyms are where you test your Pokémon against the Trainers' Pokémon.

Gym Leader (sometimes called Trainers): These are your major opponents in the game. They can be found in the gyms in the major cities. There are eight Gym Leaders and when you defeat them they will give you things, like Badges and Technical Machines. Gym Leaders are the bosses of Junior Trainers.

(Junior) Gym Leader (also called Junior Trainers): Like Gym Leaders, only not as powerful. If you have trouble with the Juniors, then it's a good idea to Level Up with some power before facing the Bosses.

Health Point (also called HP): These are the points or measurement of how healthy your Pokémon is during the game. A battle may deplete (use up) some HPs, but you can usually cure your Pokémon and get more Health Points by using a potion.

Hidden Machines (also called HM): Like Technical Machines (TM), they give your Pokémon new battle moves. However, unlike Technical Machines they can be re-used for as long as the game goes on. In fact, once a Pokémon learns a Hidden Machine skill, he has that skill forever. There are tons of Technical Machines, but only a few of the Hidden Machines. Both Technical Machines and Hidden Machines have to be given to a Pokémon type who is able to use them. A Machine for a Grass Type Pokémon will not help a Water Type very much.

Jesse/James: Two members of Team Rocket in the TV show.

Johto: The world in which the action takes place in the Gold and Silver versions. When you complete the journey in Johto, you can then move on to Kanto.

Kanto: The second world in which the action takes place in Gold and Silver versions. To reach Kanto you have to finish Johto first.

Level (also called LV or Lv): The amount of skill a Pokémon has acquired in his battles and training. The Level (or Lv) of a Pokémon will give you an idea of how well it will do against an opponent. Pokémon is different from other RPG games where the word "Level" refers to where you are in the game. For instance, the Third Level is the Magic Dragon's Dungeon. In Pokémon, the word "Level" mostly means the strength of your Pokémon character. When your Pokémon has gained enough points he can then Level Up, which means get new skills or Evolve.

Link Cable: A cable that connects to Game Boys that allows for trades and battles.

Mew: A special Pokémon that can't be caught in any version—therefore making him the rarest Pokémon. He can learn any TM or HM.

Mini Game: A smaller video game within a video game. Pokémon Stadium, for instance, has nine mini games included in it. Mini Games are usually easier to play than the main game.

Misty: In the video game she is a trainer and an opponent, but in the TV show she's one of Ash's friends. The same is true for Brock.

Mom: A new character in Gold and Silver.

NES: This means Nintendo Entertainment System. It was an earlier video game console system that ran some of the best games of its time. In Pokémon it's the game that Ash plays in his room in Pallet Town.

Oak: Also called Professor Oak. He's the world's biggest expert on Pokémon.

Pack: Not to be confused with Game Pack (or Game Pak), this item is available in the Gold and Silver versions. Basically a backpack, it comes in handy for carrying around everything you need.

Party: This is usually when a bunch of friends come over to eat cake and wear funny hats. However, when you talk about a "Pokémon Party," it usually means the group of Pokémon you've collected and are using in the game.

Pichu: A baby Pikachu that can only be found in the Gold and Silver versions.

Pikachu: Okay, Pikachu, or Pika to his friends, as just about everyone in the world already knows, is the #25 Pokémon and "Poké-star" of the game. He's also the star of the TV show, hero of countless books and a movie star. I know, I know, he's cute and deserves it all, but I remember him back when he was just an "Electric" Type.

PKMN: Means Pokémon.

Poké Ball: The thing in which you capture your Pokémon. It's round and comes in different versions: the regular Poké Ball, the Great Ball, the Ultra Ball and the Master Ball. There is also the Safari Ball, which is only good in the Safari Zone.

Pokémon: The word is Japanese and means—as if you didn't know—Pocket Monster.

Pokémon Center: Like the Poké Mart, the Poké Center is a good place for supplies . . . and more. You can find a new box at a center, plus you can heal and feed your Pokémon there. You go to the Center when you want to trade Pokémon with friends. And you can use the computers there to store and check up on your collection of Pokémon. The Pokémon Center is one of your most valuable tools in the game. Centers are located in every city.

Poké Mart: A store where a lot of different things can be bought. At a Poké Mart you can buy supplies such as Poké Balls, potions, antidotes, and other items you will need to complete the adventure.

PP: This stands for Power Points, the amount of strength you have left when in battle or about to go into battle or having just finished battle. And yes, I know what else P P is, so you can stop giggling now.

Rare Pokémon: A type of Pokémon that is difficult to find because there are not many of them. Rare Pokémon are usually only found in two places, though some are only found in one place.

Pokédex: A listing of all Pokémon that players get from Professor Oak.

Poké Gear: A device in the Pokémon Gold and Silver versions that works as a map, cell phone, radio, clock and calendar.

Pokémon Snap: (Also called just plain "Snap.") A Pokémon video game for the Nintendo 64 console system in which you track and photograph Pokémon on Pokémon Island for Professor Oak.

Pokémon Stadium: A game for the Nintendo 64 system. Players can download their Pokémon from their Game Boys into the game and get full-color, big-screen Pokémon action via the game's Transfer Pak.

Potion: A potion is a kind of medicine that can heal a Pokémon after he has been hurt in battle. Potions can be bought in the Poké Marts located all around the game. Also, potions are only one kind of medicine that Pokémon need. There are all kinds of medicines that help heal injured Pokémon. They include antidotes, burn heal, ice heal, and others.

Power Points (PP): A measure of how much power a Pokémon has. Moves require Power Points. To regain Power Points when running low, you need to go to a Poké Center.

Rare: When a Pokémon is difficult to find or can only be found in a few places, it is called "Rare."

Role Playing Game (RPG): This is a video game—like Pokémon—where you are the hero in a strange world. It is your job to walk around the world and solve problems, like collecting Pokémon. It's like exploring.

Route: The places in the game that run from one area to another. Routes are like roads (or tunnels or forests) that you must travel to get from one place to another. Lots of action takes place on these routes, so when traveling you better keep alert.

Skill: The way in which your Pokémon fights in a battle. Some Pokémon skills are learned and others are natural. A Pokémon can get skills either by reaching a certain level or by use of a Technical Machine (TM) or Hidden Machine (HM).

Satoshi Tajiri: The real inventor of Pokémon—the guy who came up with the idea for the original game. Satoshi is also the name given to the Ash character in the Japanese version.

Team Rocket: The bad guys in the TV show and the video game. In the TV show Team Rocket is made up of Jesse, James and Meowth.

TCG (means Trading Card Game): It's pretty simple really, the game is played with trading cards. So you can either just trade the cards for fun with your friends, or play the game. The cards currently come in large sets like the two-player starter set that includes two 3-card sets; the basic set that includes 102 cards; and in booster packs of 11 cards apiece.

Technical Machines (TM): Technical Machines and Hidden Machines (HM) give your Pokémon new battle moves. Technical Machines can only be used once in battle and a Pokémon can store up to four different skills at a time. Both Technical Machines and Hidden Machines have to be given to a Pokémon type who is able to use them.

Todd: The photographer character you play in Pokémon Snap. Unlike Ash, who is a kid, Todd is a teenager.

Trading: The game feature that allows you to exchange one Pokémon character for another. Some of the trading is done in the game. However, the main trading is done with two players who both have Game Boys. A cable (sold separately) connects the two units, and they can trade Pokémon back and forth. After you trade a Pokémon with a friend, you can trade back at any time.

Transfer Pack: A hardware device that comes with Pokémon Stadium that lets your Game Boy cartridge and Pokémon in it interact with your N64 system.

Types: Pokémon come in 16 different Types. These are: Normal, Grass, Water, Fire, Poison, Dragon, Ground, Rock, Flying, Psychic, Electric, Ghost, Bug, Fighting, Ice, and Bird. Bird is Missingno's Type.

Walk-Through: This is another common video game term. So you'll find it for other games, not just Pokémon. A Walk-Through is step-by-step instructions for every level of the game. Sometimes a walk-through is simply written down, and other times it may contain actual maps.

Wizards of the Coast: Also called just plain "Wizards" and "WoTC." They're the company that first came out with the Pokémon cards.

Zero-One: The land, sea and air vehicle you ride around in when you play Pokémon Snap.

it's bigger . . . it's better . . . it's funnier . . .

it's . . . the return of the ten stupidest questions ever asked about pokémon!

SINCE COMING OUT WITH THE FIRST POKÉMON book, I've had what could only be called an incredible response from kids. Hardly a day goes by when some kid doesn't come up to me and say, "I read that book. It could have been better."

Some kids are even more enthusiastic in their praise. Like last week, a fan wrote, "What's your problem, anyway? Grow up!" And then there was the comment by a real fan who wrote, "My father used your book to light the fire in the fireplace on Christmas Eve. It stunk up the house. Thanks for stinking up the house on Christmas!"

And lastly, there was the little fan who wrote an endearing letter: "I think you are as stupid as the Ten Stupidest Questions in your book! I think you are stupid, stupid, stupid, stupid and stupid . . . really stupid."

It's to these loyal fans that I dedicate the following Ten Stupidest Questions Ever Asked About Pokémon. And to all the other fans, particularly the ones who sent those packages (you know who you are), I just want to tell you that you scared everyone at the publishing house.

TEN STUPIDEST QUESTIONS

Question 1: I painted my Yellow version cartridge Gold and still can't find Lugia. Can you help?

Answer: No.

Question 2: My little brother flushed all my cards down the toilet and when the plumber came to the house, he said there was no way he could save them. Is that true?

Answer: If he could save them, would you *really* want them back? Think about it . . .

Question 3: You're stupid. How did you get that stupid? Do you go to stupid school to get stupid like you are?

Answer: I'm rubber and you are glue. Whatever you say bounces off me and sticks to you!

Question 4: What's the difference between professional wrestling and Pokémon battles?

Answer: Pokémon battles are more real than professional wrestling.

Question 5: I spent all last week during math trying to count all the Pokémon in my Pokédex and keep getting different numbers. Is there a trick to getting an accurate count?

Answer: Yes, pay attention during math class.

Question 6: There's a kid down the street that says the new Gold and

Silver games have a Pokémon that picks his nose called "Pick-an-Chew." Is Pick-an-Chew real or did he make it up?

Answer: That's made up, plus it's disgusting.

Question 7: Stupid, stupid, stupid, stupid and stupid, stupid, stupid, stupid, stupid and stupid.

Answer: That's not a question.

Question 8: I traded my sister's Backstreet Boys collection for a full set of Fossil cards and a Pikachu keychain that's only broken a little. Did I get a good deal?

Answer: Personally, I'd have to say yes, but your sister may have a different opinion.

Question 9: Can I use this book as a book report book?

Answer: No, you should only use real books for book reports.

Question 10: There's a rumor that Pokémon really live someplace in an underground lab in New Jersey. Is that true?

Answer: Yes, but the only kids who know where it is are the kids that have done their homework!

ten good pokémon questions answered

Question 1: If I never played the Red, Yellow or Blue versions will I be able to play the Gold and Silver Versions?

Answer: Yes, of course you can play the Gold and Silver versions and enjoy them. However, those kids who have experience with the Yellow, Blue and Red versions have a couple of advantages. For one thing, those earlier versions are a little easier to play. So the kids who have played Blue, Red and Yellow have a good basic understanding of the game themes and characters. Secondly, they have just played the game more and understand the tricks and gameplay a little better. On the other hand, even though it might take you a little longer to finish the game, there is no reason why you can't enjoy Gold or Silver as a first-time Pokémon player.

Question 2: The whole Clock and time thing is too complicated. Is there a way to turn off the calendar and the Clock?

Answer: I'm afraid not. The Clock and calendar are important to the game. You could say that they add another "dimension" to the game. I know, they are something else you have to think about when you're playing. But remember how difficult it was when you first started playing to think about different ways to evolve your Pokémon? How about when you thought you'd never memorize all the different Types of Pokémon, like Grass, Water and Rock? That was tough, too. A good thing to remember is that the Radio and Cell Phone give you a lot of help with the time thing.

Question 3: I never really liked playing
the Red and Blue games all the way
through to the end. I mostly liked collecting, trading Pokémon and evolving
Pokémon. Can I still play the same
way with the Gold and Silver?

Answer: Yes, absolutely. But, as you
know from your experience with the
Red and Blue versions, you still have
to play a lot of the game to get
enough Pokémon to trade and
evolve. Gold and Silver are pretty
complicated games, but there is no
reason why you can't enjoy the same
things—like trading and evolving—
that you enjoyed about the Red and
Blue versions.

Question 4: I'm having a really tough
time collecting Pokémon. It seems a lot
harder than in the first three games.

Answer: This is probably true. It may
be a lot tougher to play and catch
Pokémon. The thing to remember is
that there is a lot more stuff in the

Gold and Silver versions . . . a lot more stuff. Well, there are new Pokémon, obviously. However, there are also more types of Poke Balls, strange places to learn, and the time and date thing. The thing to remember is to use all you are given, that includes new types of Poké Balls and information from people you meet along the way and information from your Radio and Cell Phone. Also, remember, there are several basic kinds of Pokémon—those who you can catch in a certain place; those who you can only catch at a certain time, like night; and those who you can only catch after something else, some event, has happened.

Question 5: I can't find my other versions. Do I need them to get all the Pokémon?

Answer: Yes . . . But even if they are lost forever, there are still plenty of kids out there to trade with.

Question 6: Are EXP Levels just as important in the new games as the old ones?

Answer: Yep, you should try to up your Pokémon EXP levels whenever you can. This may mean taking a little Pokémon into battle to gain experience and then pulling him out again.

Question 7: I'm having a really tough time catching Marril. Is there a trick to it?

Answer: Marril is one of those Pokémon in Gold and Silver that only come out once in a while. So you'll need a tip from one of the other people you meet on the road. Always answer calls on your Cell Phone and always trade phone numbers.

Question 8: Are there any glitches in Gold and Silver like Missingno and Glitch City?

Answer: Not that I know of, but who knows, right? Both Gold and Silver are complicated games and a glitch or two might be discovered some time in the future.

Question 9: Why did they make Gold and Silver so hard to play and win?

Answer: That's easy. If the next games after Blue, Yellow and Red were easy, then kids wouldn't play them because the games wouldn't be much fun. Millions of kids learned a lot of Pokémon stuff in the first three versions. The new versions not only use that knowledge, but give you more stuff to learn and use in the game. I hate to say it, because a lot of kids will take it the wrong way, but video games like Pokémon are like school. That means, you learn something and then use it, then you learn more of the same stuff and use that and pretty soon you have the subject down cold. Suppose every class in school was the fourth grade and you just heard the same stuff over and over again for year after year? Pretty boring, huh? Each year in school should challenge you and make you think. The same is true for each new version of a video game.

Question 10: I know a kid who has parents who won't let him play Pokémon. I think that's really stupid, he's just going to come over to my house to play.

Answer: No, that's not stupid. You should respect the rules of your friend's parents. Offering to let him play any video game that his parents don't allow him to play at home is disrespectful to his parents. And you just shouldn't do it.

pokémon are stars!

"I liked the First Movie a lot. My mom hated it. She didn't like it. I think it made my mind think. It wasn't a boring movie. Surprisingly, a kid next to me started crying at the end. I saw it and he was crying. I guess to some people the ending of the first movie was a tear jerker. I thought it was just like really interesting."

—Colin

ADULTS JUST DON'T "GET IT," BUT KIDS LOVE IT. Try watching the Pokémon movie some time on the home VCR and watch parents find an excuse to leave the room.

"I can't watch TV now, sorry, I'm expecting a call about finding out if I'm happy with my long-distance service," a parent will say. "I'm sorry, I've been waiting all week to talk to someone about long-distance service."

But is it any surprise that they just don't get it?

First of all, they don't know any of the characters. And, they don't know how the game is played. Plus, the drawing style of the cartoon—I know, it's really called *animé*—is a whole lot different than American cartoons (and yes, I know they're called animation!).

To help kids out, I would suggest that they remind their parents about some of the first animé shows on TV. These were great old shows that maybe even your parents watched or still watch. There was Astro Boy and Tobor, the Eighth Man. Then there was Speed Racer and Gigantor. Speed Racer was about a kid race car driver and his friends, which included a pet monkey. And Gigantor was a giant robot.

Race car drivers with pet monkeys and giant robots? Yep . . . and you can bet that your parent's parents didn't "get it" either!

Now we're into a whole new series of Pokémon. The new series debuted at around the same time that the Gold and Silver versions came out. And, in case you didn't know, the series is called: The Johto Journeys.

What that means is that all the new Pokémon from the new games will be included in the new series. Right now, there are over 100 episodes of the TV show with more on the way. Plus, they include all of the characters from the first round of shows.

"The second movie was better. It had more adventure in it. It was just more interesting. There was a favorite part when Lugia was using his element blast. It was really cool. He was so powerful." **—Greg**

"I don't think the first movie was as good as it seemed when I first saw it. I saw it on its opening night. I thought the story line was really bad. What I look for in a movie is a good story line. You gotta make the best part when the good guys defeat the bad guys. You gotta make that interesting and a lot of fun to watch. The action scenes [in the first movie] were really not that good." **—Adam**

"The first movie, I thought it stunk, frankly. It just had no meaning. It made no sense and it jumped around. Also, everybody already knew about Mew and Mewtwo, so all of a sudden we're finding out about Mew and Mewtwo? It was very confusing and stupid. The only reason I wanted to see it was because you got free Pokémon cards. The Pokémon cards were really good." **—Nina**

Pokémon: The First Movie

I, personally, thought that the first movie was pretty good. I know a lot of kids that didn't like the little short about Pikachu's Vacation, but it was something extra and if you didn't like it, then you could always go out and get more popcorn or something. It didn't last long.

For those who missed the first movie in the theaters and maybe are thinking of renting it, it's definitely worth renting. The plot goes something like this: Ash, Pikachu and a bunch of friends are invited to a mysterious island. Once there, they find that they have been tricked into a huge battle they may not be prepared to handle with the world's most powerful and fierce Pokémon.

> "Pikachu's Vacation . . . What I liked about it is that Pikachu got to do whatever he wanted to and he got a vacation day to himself. He's my favorite Pokémon so he deserved a good day of rest."
> **—Stuart**

Pokémon the Movie 2000

The second movie is called *Pokémon the Movie 2000*. It's not exactly a sequel to the first movie, but I have to say that it's definitely better. This time Ash Ketchum and his friends have to save the whole Earth from destruction. In the first movie, audiences got to see a new Pokémon, and the same is true for the second movie. And in this film there are even more new Pokémon introduced.

Will parents like the second movie better than the first movie? Probably not. But the real question is, will kids like the second movie more than the first movie? And I'd have to say definitely. It's a really, really good Pokémon movie.

"When Lugia came out of the water in the second movie it was pretty cool because he's my favorite Pokémon. I expected to see Lugia but I didn't know when I was going to see him. I didn't expect him to come out at that minute. In the first movie, my favorite part is in the beginning when Mewtwo joins Giovanni because Mewtwo is one of my former favorite Pokémon and Giovanni is probably my favorite character. Not that I don't like Mewtwo anymore. It's just that I haven't seen it very much, only in that movie. He's probably the strongest Pokémon. I like Giovanni because he's sort of like a leader of an evil organization." **—Will**

"Pikachu's Rescue Adventure, I liked that. I liked when Pikachu, Snorlax, Eeevee and all of Ash's Pokémon rescued Togepi. He also rescued five nests of eggs. It was a big storm and it was about to blow all of them away and Bulbasaur tied the vines onto the nests. And then the wind started to blow them away. All of Ash's Pokémon pulled on him and all of Ash's Pokémon were about to blow away. And then Snorlax came and then he saved all of them. He was about to let

them blow away. He let go of them because
he stopped to eat an apple. Then he saved
them."   **–David**

pokémon tv

and something to think about

"The early parts of the TV show and the Orange Islands aren't that fun to watch anymore. The Johto Journeys rock!" **—Jason**

WHEN POKÉMON BECAME SUCH A HUGE HIT ON TV, the folks in television realized that American kids would watch animé. It didn't matter that the eyes of the characters were huge and that the art was a lot different than American cartoons. Kids loved them.

After Pokémon came Digimon, Gundam Wing and a lot of other shows. After all, the shows were big hits in Japan and now they were big hits in the U.S.

Suddenly animé was everywhere. You could turn on the TV before school or after school and on Saturday morning and see an animé show. This is pretty cool. It's pretty cool to think about kids in Japan and kids in the U.S. liking the same shows.

There are also a few things you should know about animé. For one thing, Japanese cartoons are a lot like American cartoons in some ways. For instance, a lot of Japanese cartoons get their start in comic books. The same is true for American cartoons, like Superman, Batman and even Men in Black. All of these American cartoons got their start in comic books.

Another thing that's interesting about animé is that it's just not for kids. They have animé action/adventures, science fiction, romances and even animé soap operas in Japan. Adults, kids and teenagers all watch animé.

If you like shows like Pokémon and Digimon, you might want to check out your local video store for some other animé titles. After all, there are a lot of movies and shows out there that weren't made into video games. And some of them are very, very good.

A NOTE TO PARENTS

As I mentioned above, there are a great

many animé—Japanese animation—titles
available for rental and purchase. However, parents should take care to pre-screen
these films and shows. In Japan animé is
not considered only a kid's entertainment.
Many of these titles deal with adult themes
and may contain unacceptable levels of
violence.

catch list for gold, silver, blue and red

HERE'S A HANDY CATCH LIST FOR YOU TO KEEP track when you're away from your Game Boy. Simply put a check mark or cross out the Pokémon as you catch them. Some of them have notes beside them to remind you of some important feature.

1.	**Bulbasaur**	◯ CAUGHT
2.	**Ivysaur**	◯ CAUGHT
3.	**Venusaur**	◯ CAUGHT
4.	**Charmander**	◯ CAUGHT
5.	**Charmeleon**	◯ CAUGHT

6.	*Charizard*	◯ CAUGHT
7.	*Squirtle*	◯ CAUGHT
8.	*Wartortle*	◯ CAUGHT
9.	*Blastoise*	◯ CAUGHT
10.	*Caterpie*	◯ CAUGHT
11.	*Metapod*	◯ CAUGHT
12.	*Butterfree*	◯ CAUGHT
13.	*Weedle*	◯ CAUGHT
14.	*Kakuna*	◯ CAUGHT
15.	*Beedrill*	◯ CAUGHT
16.	*Pidgey*	◯ CAUGHT
17.	*Pidgeotto*	◯ CAUGHT

18.	**Pidgeot**	◯ CAUGHT
19.	**Rattata**	◯ CAUGHT
20.	**Raticate**	◯ CAUGHT
21.	**Spearow**	◯ CAUGHT
22.	**Fearow**	◯ CAUGHT
23.	**Ekans**	◯ CAUGHT
24.	**Arbok**	◯ CAUGHT
25.	**Pikachu**	◯ CAUGHT
26.	**Raichu**	◯ CAUGHT
27.	**Sandshrew**	◯ CAUGHT
28.	**Sandslash**	◯ CAUGHT
29.	**Nidoran (F)**	◯ CAUGHT

30.	**Nidorina**	◯ CAUGHT
31.	**Nidoqueen**	◯ CAUGHT
32.	**Nidoran (M)**	◯ CAUGHT
33.	**Nidorino**	◯ CAUGHT
34.	**Nidoking**	◯ CAUGHT
35.	**Clefairy**	◯ CAUGHT
36.	**Clefable**	◯ CAUGHT
37.	**Vulpix** ONLY IN SILVER	◯ CAUGHT
38.	**Ninetales** ONLY IN SILVER	◯ CAUGHT
39.	**Jigglypuff**	◯ CAUGHT
40.	**Wigglytuff**	◯ CAUGHT
41.	**Zubat**	◯ CAUGHT

42.	**Golbat**	○ CAUGHT
43.	**Oddish**	○ CAUGHT
44.	**Gloom**	○ CAUGHT
45.	**Vileplume**	○ CAUGHT
46.	**Paras**	○ CAUGHT
47.	**Parasect**	○ CAUGHT
48.	**Venonat**	○ CAUGHT
49.	**Venomoth**	○ CAUGHT
50.	**Diglett**	○ CAUGHT
51.	**Dugtrio**	○ CAUGHT
52.	**Meowth** ONLY IN SILVER	○ CAUGHT
53.	**Persian** ONLY IN SILVER	○ CAUGHT

54.	**Psyduck**	◯ CAUGHT
55.	**Golduck**	◯ CAUGHT
56.	**Mankey** *ONLY IN GOLD*	◯ CAUGHT
57.	**Primeape** *ONLY IN GOLD*	◯ CAUGHT
58.	**Growlithe** *ONLY IN GOLD*	◯ CAUGHT
59.	**Arcanine** *ONLY IN GOLD*	◯ CAUGHT
60.	**Poliwag**	◯ CAUGHT
61.	**Poliwhirl**	◯ CAUGHT
62.	**Poliwrath**	◯ CAUGHT
63.	**Abra**	◯ CAUGHT
64.	**Kadabra**	◯ CAUGHT
65.	**Alakazam**	◯ CAUGHT

66.	**Machop**	◯ CAUGHT
67.	**Machoke**	◯ CAUGHT
68.	**Machamp**	◯ CAUGHT
69.	**Bellsprout**	◯ CAUGHT
70.	**Weepinbell**	◯ CAUGHT
71.	**Victreebel**	◯ CAUGHT
72.	**Tentacool**	◯ CAUGHT
73.	**Tentacruel**	◯ CAUGHT
74.	**Geodude**	◯ CAUGHT
75.	**Graveler**	◯ CAUGHT
76.	**Golem**	◯ CAUGHT
77.	**Ponyta**	◯ CAUGHT

78.	**Rapidash**	◯ CAUGHT
79.	**Slowpoke**	◯ CAUGHT
80.	**Slowbro**	◯ CAUGHT
81.	**Magnemite**	◯ CAUGHT
82.	**Magneton**	◯ CAUGHT
83.	**Farfetch'd**	◯ CAUGHT
84.	**Doduo**	◯ CAUGHT
85.	**Dodrio**	◯ CAUGHT
86.	**Seel**	◯ CAUGHT
87.	**Dewgong**	◯ CAUGHT
88.	**Grimer**	◯ CAUGHT
89.	**Muk**	◯ CAUGHT

90.	**Shellder**	◯ CAUGHT
91.	**Cloyster**	◯ CAUGHT
92.	**Gastly**	◯ CAUGHT
93.	**Haunter**	◯ CAUGHT
94.	**Gengar**	◯ CAUGHT
95.	**Onix**	◯ CAUGHT
96.	**Drowzee**	◯ CAUGHT
97.	**Hypno**	◯ CAUGHT
98.	**Krabby**	◯ CAUGHT
99.	**Kingler**	◯ CAUGHT
100.	**Voltorb**	◯ CAUGHT
101.	**Electrode**	◯ CAUGHT

102.	**Exeggcute**	○ CAUGHT
103.	**Exeggutor**	○ CAUGHT
104.	**Cubone**	○ CAUGHT
105.	**Marowak**	○ CAUGHT
106.	**Hitmonlee**	○ CAUGHT
107.	**Hitmonchan**	○ CAUGHT
108.	**Likitung**	○ CAUGHT
109.	**Koffing**	○ CAUGHT
110.	**Weezing**	○ CAUGHT
111.	**Rhyhorn**	○ CAUGHT
112.	**Rhydon**	○ CAUGHT
113.	**Chansey**	○ CAUGHT

114.	**Tangela**	◯ CAUGHT
115.	**Kangaskhan**	◯ CAUGHT
116.	**Horsea**	◯ CAUGHT
117.	**Seadra**	◯ CAUGHT
118.	**Goldeen**	◯ CAUGHT
119.	**Seaking**	◯ CAUGHT
120.	**Staryu**	◯ CAUGHT
121.	**Starmie**	◯ CAUGHT
122.	**Mr. Mime**	◯ CAUGHT
123.	**Scyther**	◯ CAUGHT
124.	**Jynx**	◯ CAUGHT
125.	**Electabuzz**	◯ CAUGHT

126.	**Magmar**	◯ CAUGHT
127.	**Pinsir**	◯ CAUGHT
128.	**Tauros**	◯ CAUGHT
129.	**Magikarp**	◯ CAUGHT
130.	**Gyarados**	◯ CAUGHT
131.	**Lapras**	◯ CAUGHT
132.	**Ditto**	◯ CAUGHT
133.	**Eevee**	◯ CAUGHT
134.	**Vaporeon**	◯ CAUGHT
135.	**Jolteon**	◯ CAUGHT
136.	**Flareon**	◯ CAUGHT
137.	**Porygon**	◯ CAUGHT

138.	**Omanyte**	◯ CAUGHT
139.	**Omastar**	◯ CAUGHT
140.	**Kabuto**	◯ CAUGHT
141.	**Kabutops**	◯ CAUGHT
142.	**Aerodactyl**	◯ CAUGHT
143.	**Snorlax**	◯ CAUGHT
144.	**Articuno**	◯ CAUGHT
145.	**Zapdos**	◯ CAUGHT
146.	**Moltres**	◯ CAUGHT
147.	**Dratini**	◯ CAUGHT
148.	**Dragonair**	◯ CAUGHT
149.	**Dragonite**	◯ CAUGHT

150.	**Mewtwo**	◯ CAUGHT
151.	**Mew**	◯ CAUGHT
152.	**Chikorita**	◯ CAUGHT
153.	**Bayleef**	◯ CAUGHT
154.	**Meganium**	◯ CAUGHT
155.	**Cyndaquil**	◯ CAUGHT
156.	**Quilava**	◯ CAUGHT
157.	**Typhlosion**	◯ CAUGHT
158.	**Totodile**	◯ CAUGHT
159.	**Croconaw**	◯ CAUGHT
160.	**Feraligatr**	◯ CAUGHT
161.	**Sentret**	◯ CAUGHT

162.	**Furret**	○ CAUGHT
163.	**Hoothoot**	○ CAUGHT
164.	**Noctowl**	○ CAUGHT
165.	**Ledyba** ONLY IN SILVER	○ CAUGHT
166.	**Ledian** ONLY IN SILVER	○ CAUGHT
167.	**Spinarak** ONLY IN GOLD	○ CAUGHT
168.	**Ariados** ONLY IN GOLD	○ CAUGHT
169.	**Kurobat**	○ CAUGHT
170.	**Chinchou**	○ CAUGHT
171.	**Lanturn**	○ CAUGHT
172.	**Pichu** BABY POKÉMON	○ CAUGHT
173.	**Cleffa** BABY POKÉMON	○ CAUGHT

174.	**Igglybuff** BABY POKÉMON	◯ CAUGHT
175.	**Togepi**	◯ CAUGHT
176.	**Togetic**	◯ CAUGHT
177.	**Natu**	◯ CAUGHT
178.	**Xatu**	◯ CAUGHT
179.	**Mareep**	◯ CAUGHT
180.	**Flaaffy**	◯ CAUGHT
181.	**Denryuu**	◯ CAUGHT
182.	**Bellosom**	◯ CAUGHT
183.	**Marril**	◯ CAUGHT
184.	**Azumarril**	◯ CAUGHT
185.	**Sudowoodo**	◯ CAUGHT

186.	**Politoed**	◯ CAUGHT
187.	**Hoppip**	◯ CAUGHT
188.	**Skiploom**	◯ CAUGHT
189.	**Jumpluff**	◯ CAUGHT
190.	**Aipom**	◯ CAUGHT
191.	**Sunkern**	◯ CAUGHT
192.	**Sunflora**	◯ CAUGHT
193.	**Dunsparce**	◯ CAUGHT
194.	**Ampharos**	◯ CAUGHT
195.	**Quagsire**	◯ CAUGHT
196.	**Espeon**	◯ CAUGHT
197.	**Umbreon**	◯ CAUGHT

198.	**Murkrow**	○ CAUGHT
199.	**Slowking**	○ CAUGHT
200.	**Trillix**	○ CAUGHT
201.	**Unown**	○ CAUGHT
202.	**Wobbuffet**	○ CAUGHT
203.	**Girafarig**	○ CAUGHT
204.	**Skarmory** *ONLY IN SILVER*	○ CAUGHT
205.	**Forrestress**	○ CAUGHT
206.	**Duglari**	○ CAUGHT
207.	**Gligar** *ONLY IN GOLD*	○ CAUGHT
208.	**Steelix**	○ CAUGHT
209.	**Snubbull**	○ CAUGHT

210.	**Granbull**	◯ CAUGHT
211.	**Quilfish**	◯ CAUGHT
212.	**Scizor**	◯ CAUGHT
213.	**Schuckle**	◯ CAUGHT
214.	**Heracross**	◯ CAUGHT
215.	**Misdreavus**	◯ CAUGHT
216.	**Teddiursa**	◯ CAUGHT
217.	**Ursaring**	◯ CAUGHT
218.	**Slugma**	◯ CAUGHT
219.	**Magcargo**	◯ CAUGHT
220.	**Swinub**	◯ CAUGHT
221.	**Piloswine**	◯ CAUGHT

222.	**Corsola**	○ CAUGHT
223.	**Remoraid**	○ CAUGHT
224.	**Octillery**	○ CAUGHT
225.	**Delibird** *ONLY IN SILVER*	○ CAUGHT
226.	**Mantine**	○ CAUGHT
227.	**Wooper**	○ CAUGHT
228.	**Houndour**	○ CAUGHT
229.	**Houndoom**	○ CAUGHT
230.	**Kingdra**	○ CAUGHT
231.	**Phanpy**	○ CAUGHT
232.	**Donphan** *ONLY IN SILVER*	○ CAUGHT
233.	**Porygon 2**	○ CAUGHT

234.	**Stantler** *ONLY IN SILVER*	○ CAUGHT
235.	**Smeargle**	○ CAUGHT
236.	**Tyrogue**	○ CAUGHT
237.	**Hitmontop**	○ CAUGHT
238.	**Smoochum** *BABY POKÉMON*	○ CAUGHT
239.	**Elekid** *BABY POKÉMON*	○ CAUGHT
240.	**Magby** *BABY POKÉMON*	○ CAUGHT
241.	**Milktank**	○ CAUGHT
242.	**Blissey**	○ CAUGHT
243.	**Raikou**	○ CAUGHT
244.	**Entei**	○ CAUGHT
245.	**Suicune**	○ CAUGHT

246.	**Larvitar**	◯ CAUGHT
247.	**Pupitar**	◯ CAUGHT
248.	**Tyranitar**	◯ CAUGHT
249.	**Lugia**	◯ CAUGHT
250.	**Ho-oh**	◯ CAUGHT
251.	**Selebi**	◯ CAUGHT

what's gonna be new . . . soon!

IN CASE YOU HAVEN'T HEARD YET, THERE'S A NEW Game Boy coming out. It's called Game Boy Advance. Since Game Boy was first sold to U.S. kids in the late 1980s, the company has sold more than 100 million of them around the world. That's a lot of games. Naturally the system has changed, the biggest so far being Game Boy Color. And there've been other hand-held video games—but Game Boy is still the most popular.

Now, with the Game Boy Advance, we're going to see some real action. Why is that? I think because of two reasons. The first reason is that before Pokémon, hand-held games were kind of "ho-hum . . . what a yawn." Sure, kids played them, but they only played them when they couldn't get to a console game with larger screen and better graphics and sound. And, let's face it, Pokémon for the original Game Boy didn't have great graphics, great sound and you better believe it didn't have a large screen . . . all it had was truly phenomenal game play. And that was enough to make it a hit.

Before Pokémon there wasn't a huge, mega-hit blockbuster game for hand-helds. Most of the games were stripped-down versions of console games.

So you can believe that the folks at Nintendo and the video game designers outside Nintendo are really looking to do something special for the new Game Boy Advance. Hand-helds are "ho-hum" no more.

The second reason is that the technology has gotten so much better. This trend in computers—and yes, Game Boys are like little computers because they have a silicon chip in them and work about the same way as a computer—has been going on for a long time. More than 30 years, in fact. It was first noticed by a guy named Gordon Moore, one of the co-founders of

Intel, a company that makes computer chips.

Moore—let's call him Gordon!—realized that every year or so computer chips got faster and smaller. That's because the number of transistors companies could fit on a chip doubled every year. He called this "Moore's Law," which is probably better than "Gordon's Law" or "Gordie's Law."

So, here's the way Moore's Law has worked in computers. Take a penny and put it in a jar. The next day, put two pennies in a jar. And the next day put four pennies in a jar. Double the number of pennies you put in the jar for a month. Those pennies will really add up. So did the computer power . . . in the 1970s when computer chips were just getting going, there were only a couple of thousand transistors on the chips. Today, there are millions of transistors on a computer chip . . . millions! That means the chip is fast . . . *really* fast!

HEY, THIS SOUNDS LIKE SCHOOL . . . WHAT ABOUT THE NEW GAME BOY?

Sorry, I thought you might enjoy a little education . . .

What this means for the new Game Boy is that it will have more processing power that the previous Game Boys. And more processing power means you can do a lot more stuff . . . that the game designers can do a lot more stuff.

For instance, the Game Boy Color has an 8-bit chip in it and the Game Boy Advance has a 32-bit chip in it. You do the math on that one.

Other features that the Advance may have are a lot more simultaneous colors on the screen. That means better graphics. And to support those better graphics, the company has made the screen larger.

And there's another change. The GB Advance (now being called the GBA by some people) has a horizontal format. Place your vertical Color Game Boy on its side and you'll get the idea. Naturally, all the controls have been moved around so you can play it in the new format.

There's also word that it will allow for multi-player play by linking the GBA up with cables, like you do with Pokémon, plus you'll probably be able to link it to

Nintendo's new console system, which hasn't been released, either.

SO, WHAT DOES ALL THIS MEAN, ANYWAY?

Glad you asked . . . It means that handhelds, which were once boring, are here to stay in a big, big way. Computer chips are cheaper, kids like playing them, and companies know they can make games that kids will play on them.

It also means that companies will probably get more creative with hand-helds and cartridges. Think about it . . . there has been more cool stuff with hand-helds in just the last couple of years than all the previous years put together . . . most of this, of course, was done by Nintendo. Pokémon Pinball had a little rumble pak in it. Pokémon Stadium lets you download from a hand-held. Then there's the Game Boy Camera and printer . . . so who knows what's coming next? Those are some powerful chips that will be in the new Game Boy, so a lot is possible. It'll just take some imagination . . .

tim's glitch city and missingno chapter

HEY, WHO IS TIM AND WHY DOES HE HAVE HIS own chapter?

Glad you asked. Tim's one of the kids who has been contributing to these books since the beginning. Even before I started writing this book, he was sending me stuff on Glitch City. He was that anxious that everyone know about it.

Soon he was calling me. Five, eight, even thirty times a day, asking if I'd written the Glitch City chapter yet. When I stopped picking up the phone he would shout into the answering machine: "I KNOW WHERE YOU LIVE!!!"

Okay, that last part isn't true. He didn't call and threaten me. He's actually a good kid. And if anyone is a Pokémon Master, it's Tim.

And right now he's really into Missingno and Glitch City. So I figured I'd give him his own chapter. This one's for you, Tim.

The first thing you should know is that Glitch City and Missingno only appear in the Red, Blue and Yellow versions (there is another Missingno in Stadium, but not the original). However, a lot of kids, like Tim, have been getting deeper into the game after they've collected all the Pokémon and finished the game.

Secondly, both Glitch City and Missingno are not official parts of the game. They are, well, glitches—mistakes in the programming.

"PLEASE, ALL OF YOU READERS! YOU MUST TRY THIS!"–Tim

To activate Glitch City follow these simple steps. You must have Pokémon that know HM02 and HM03.

1) Go into Safari Zone's entrance building and when the guy says, "It's $500 to enter, would you like to come in?" say "Yes."

2) Then go into the first rest house you encounter. Talk to the guy in the glasses once, then leave early.

3) When the guy says, "Leaving early?" Say "No." You will be sent back out. Don't make a move.

4) After doing this, leave early again, and when the guy says, "Leaving early?" say "No" again.

5) Once you are back in Safari Zone, save the game, turn it off, then turn it back on. After you do this, leave early again.

6) Once you leave early again, this is when the first glitch appears. Instead of the guy saying, "Leaving early?" he says, "It's $500 to enter. Would you like to come in?" Say "No."

7) From there you will be sent back to Fuschia. Pretty normal, huh? Well, the code's not over! Once in Fuschia fly to Cinnabar Island. Then surf up and down the east coast. You will not find Missingno. You will run into Safari Pokémon. Now this may take about ten minutes, but it works. The amount of time you have to catch Pokémon in the Safari Zone will be the same on Cinnabar Island. It takes about 500 steps until time is up, so if you'd like to keep track, just count 500 steps. And when you run into Safari Pokémon, just run away. It doesn't change anything. Trust me, it does work!

After 500 steps, you will hear a "Ding-Dong" just like you hear in the Safari Zone when you run out of time, only it's on Cinnabar Island. You will automatically be transported to the Safari Zone entrance building. When you leave the building you will be in Glitch City!

Warning: Don't go far to the left or you will get stuck in invisible walls and not get out.

8) Glitch City is also entirely safe. It will not mess up your game!

9) Glitch City works in the Yellow version!

"The only way to get out of Glitch City is to fly with an HM2."   **–Maxwell**

GLITCH CITY CORRUPTION

Here is something to do if you get to Glitch City and have nothing else to do. When you come out of the Safari Zone, you will be in Glitch City. Then go a little ways to the left until you encounter a hedge. Jump over it. Then, go down to the checkered water. Go to the top-left water square. From there, go left one space, and then go right one space. You will be stuck. Then surf on that one square of water. You will be surfing on land! After surfing on land, you can surf to the right. If you surf to the right too far, the screen will glitch and then black out. You will not be able to play, but your game will NOT be erased. Just turn the power off and then on. But . . . we do not recommend doing this on Game Boy Tower in Pokémon Stadium. A screen appears that says "Corruption."

MISSINGNO

Missingno is a glitch in the game. If you catch it, it may mess up your game—but not permanently. It goes away after a while, even after catching it—but your Pokémon League will always be messed up. I caught six Missingnos without my game being erased—this is true! However, if you don't want the "Missingno Virus" in your game, just release Missingno and the defects will go away.

The major way to cause the "Missingno Virus" is to look at Missingno or M's stats. So, Tim, how exactly do you catch Missingno?

Fly to north Viridian City. Ask the guy with the coffee and say "No." Watch him catch a Pokémon, then fly down to Cinnabar Island. Swim along the east coast and you will find him. Sometimes he will be called "M." It is true that M is safer to catch than Missingno because M *does* evolve into Kangaskhan. This is not a rumor. Once you run into Missingno and you have Master Ball, Rare Candy, or Nuggets as your sixth item you will get a glitch-kind of symbol next to that item. That means you have about 150 of them.

TIM'S MISSINGNO FACTS

Missingno is #000: No wonder he's called Missingno. It means Missing Number!

His attacks are two Water Guns and a Sky Attack.

The only known TMs he can learn are TM01 (Mega-Punch); TM02 (Razor Wind); TM05 (Mega Kick); TM14 (Blizzard); and TM49 (Tri Attack).

Missingno canNOT learn TM23, TM15, and TM50.

The only HM he can learn is HM02 (fly).

Also, Missingno will have a very high attack power, but low in defense, speed and special. Missingno's Types are Bird and Normal.

TRADING MISSINGNO
Do you know how when you look at your party and you see these weird little figures next to each Pokémon's name? Well, Missingno's little figure is a man-shaped figure. When you trade Missingno into the Yellow version, it will look like a Wishbone. Also, when it's in the Yellow version, its name will be a bunch of gibberish and it will be #176!

MORE MISSINGNO FACTS FROM TIM
When you are battling with Missingno and you see the back of a Pokémon's head, Missingno looks like a random block of static. Also, when you have Missingno, most of the time all of the Pokémon and trainers you meet will be

backwards. And once you use an attack on them, their bodies will get slicked up in glitch.

MISSINGNO AND POKÉMON STADIUM

Missingno looks like a substitute in Pokémon Stadium. There is bad news about putting Missingno into the Pokémon Stadium. Not that your game will glitch or anything, but it's just that you can't use it in battle. You can take photo shots of it in the Gallery, but the photos don't appear when developed. Finally, if you put it in Prof. Oak's lab, look at its stats, and everything will be "?". And if you look at it in your party list, your game will freeze.

* * *

SPECIAL BONUS "HEY YOU, PIKACHU" SECTION BY TIM

Hey, what is this "Hey You, Pikachu" anyway? "Hey You, Pikachu" is, so far, the most futuristic N64 game. Why? Because you actually get to *talk* to Pikachu in the game! The game has what's called a VRS

(Voice Recognition System), which is a microphone that lets you talk into the game. Pikachu acts as a virtual pet. And it is in stores now!!

TIPS FOR THIS NEW GAME:

- If Pikachu understands what you have said, the microphone icon in the screen will light up.

- There are mini games throughout the game, just as in Pokémon Stadium. One is that you have to go get Pikachu some food by throwing balls and hitting a tree to get apples.

- Pikachu has emotions—sad, scared, mad, happy, surprised, and even embarrassed! If you say "You're cute," Pikachu will blush, but if you fling curses at him, the little yellow Pokémon will shock you.

In *Pokémon Fever* it was announced that "Hey You, Pikachu" would never come to America. That turned out to be incorrect. Finally, "Hey You, Pikachu" has come to America!

are pokémon cards still cool?

THE ANSWER TO THAT IS "YES. POKÉMON CARDS are still cool." For one thing, it would be darned difficult to play the strategy game without them, right?

I know that some kids have given up on collecting and trading the cards. Or, if they are still collecting and trading, then they aren't doing it as much. This is partly because many kids' collections are filling up.

"I used to collect Pokémon cards. But now, I only need seven cards to have a complete set of 151, so I am still on the lookout for those seven cards." **–Raymond**

It's probably a good thing, because it was getting really crazy there for a while. A lot of schools banned the cards. And some kids got into fights over the cards. Remember all that stuff?

No, kids aren't acting so crazy about Pokémon cards anymore. And whenever people don't act crazy, I think that's a good thing . . . but that may just be me. In my opinion, kids act crazy enough without the card thing making them even nuttier.

So, if you like the strategy game, keep playing it. If you like collecting and trading, keep collecting and trading. Hint: With so many kids no longer acting crazy about the cards, you can probably make some great trades now.

Another thing a lot of kids ask me is, "Why aren't the cards so popular anymore?" The answer to that is, I think that a lot of kids just got caught up in all the excitement and when the excitement died down, they moved on to other things. Another reason I think is that the kids collecting and trading the cards did it for the excitement of collecting and trading. And that was definitely one part of it, but not all of it. And, thirdly, I think that for the collecting, trading and Game Boy playing kids, the cards served another purpose. For those kids, the cards taught them about the different Pokémon, the Evolutions and Types and all the rest. Once they learned all of that, then they no longer needed the cards.

And yeah, the cards are still cool if you still like them.

"One trade I've made with my friend was his Dragonite for my Vaporeon. They were both holographic." **—Jason**

GOOD NEWS ABOUT CARDS . . .

If you like collecting the cards, there is good news. There are more companies than ever making different types of cards. Topps, Wizards of the Coast, and other types that are promotional. Plus, there are Chase cards and more Holos to collect as well. This is all good news. New packs are still being issued and a lot of kids are still buying them.

Also, now that the craze has turned not so crazy, the cards are not only easier to get, but there seems to be fewer counterfeit cards around. This is all good news.

And lastly, not too many stores are asking

huge prices for cards now. That means that you—as a smart collector—can shop around and get the card you want at a fair price.

> *"My favorite cards are Ancient Mew, American Mew, American Dragonite, Holographic Ditto, and Holographic American Charizard. I like them because they are rare, and when in card battles, they are very powerful."* **—Tim**

AND SOME BAD NEWS ABOUT CARDS

Remember how you thought you had a fortune in cards? Well, you probably don't. I've heard that a first print run of Charizard is still pretty rare, but let's face it, all those kids who thought they were going to get rich by trading cards are not rich.

> *"Once someone bought a Dark Blastoise in Japanese for $900! And I was there the moment he bought it!"* **—Aaron**

The truth of the matter is—from what I've heard and read—that the only people who made a lot of money on the Pokémon cards were the store owners who charged extremely high prices for the cards when everybody wanted them.

dumb facts for free

THIS SPECIAL BONUS SECTION IS CALLED DUMB Facts for Free. These facts will not help you do better in school. They won't even help you play the game more. And, probably, filling up your brain with dumb facts like these will make you less smart.

So why did I include a Dumb Facts for Free section? Hey, they're free.

Nintendo sold 1.4 million copies of Gold and Silver in the U.S. the first week it went on sale. That's enough to give the about 800,000 people who live in San Francisco one and three-quarters game cartridges each—whether they want the cartridges or not!

Then, if you took all of those 1.4 million cartridges—measuring about two and a half inches—and put them end to end, they would stretch 55 miles. If that doesn't sound like a lot, do this experiment: next time you are traveling 55 mph in a car for an hour, imagine the cartridges are lined up along the highway. That's a lot of video games! And that's only what kids bought the first week.

Now, if you figure that each kid took one of the cartridges home and played it for ten hours the first weekend, then that's 14 million hours of video games. How long is 14 million hours? Glad you asked!

There are 8,760 hours in a year. So all the kids playing the 1.4 million cartridges for the first weekend played more than 159 years of video game. If you went back into history 159 years, it means that they played video games back to before Abraham Lincoln was President of the U.S. And if I'm not right about this . . . then I'm obviously wrong. Right?

I know what you're saying about now. You're saying, "Hey, what a cheap way to trick somebody into doing math! What a cheap trick!"

So what if it was a cheap trick, it worked, right? Try it with some other large number and see what you can come up with . . . it's actually pretty cool.

the end (really!)

I WANT TO SAY THAT I'VE HAD A GREAT TIME writing all three of the Pokémon guides. The kids who helped out are great. And the letters that I've gotten about the books are also great—I've done my best to try and answer them.

Also, I hope that you've enjoyed reading the books, even the goofy jokes, and maybe gotten a laugh or two out of them.

Thanks, guys.

LOOK FOR

How to Win at Nintendo® 64 Games #2

AND

Sony Playstation 2: The Unauthorized Guide

—BOTH FROM HANK SCHLESINGER
AND ST. MARTIN'S PAPERBACKS!

FIND OUT EVERYTHING YOU NEED
TO KNOW TO MASTER
THE WORLD'S FAVORITE
HAND-HELD GAME

HOW TO BECOME A POKÉMON MASTER

By Hank Schlesinger

It's all here. Amaze your friends, astound your parents, and impress your classmates with the valuable expert tips that can turn you into a champion Pokémon player. And you'll get them straight from the source: kids just like you who have played for hours on end and discovered the amazing secrets of this awesome game! Author Hank Schlesinger—an avid video game junkie himself—has interviewed kids who love Pokémon, and thrown in his own insights and tips, to create the ultimate Pokémon guide.

WITH SPECIAL BONUS TIPS FOR
OTHER GAME BOY GAMES

**An Unauthorized Guide—
Not Endorsed by Nintendo**

AVAILABLE WHEREVER BOOKS ARE SOLD
FROM ST. MARTIN'S PAPERBACKS

Pokémon Art Page

DRAW YOUR FAVORITE POKÉMON CHARACTER HERE!